Slaughterhouse Rules

One Man's Success in Navigating Life, Hollywood, and the

Corporate World

James M. Myers

Published in the United States of America by SHR Publishing

Design by Kearby Milliner, Jean Ashenfelter
Photography by Sunny Mays

Library of Congress Cataloging-in-Publication Data
Slaughterhouse rules : one man's success in navigating life, Hollywood, and the corporate world / James M. Myers.
SHR Publishing, [2017]
ISBN 978-0-9982818-3-4 (hardcover) | ISBN 978-0-9982818-1-0 (paperback) | ISBN 978-0-9982818-0-3 (ebook) | ISBN 978-0-9982818-2-7 (ePub)
Actors--United States--Biography. | Businesspeople--United States--Biography. | Self-actualization (Psychology) | Life change events. | Success. | LCGFT: Autobiographies.
Classification: LCC PN2287.M94 A3 2017 (print) | LCC PN2287.M94 (ebook) | DDC 791.4302/8092--dc23

ISBN: 978-0-9982818-4-1

PREFACE

Sitting at the bar in the country club this past summer, a golfing colleague was listening to me tell him about my crazy life experiences. He gave me a single piece of feedback, "You should write a book." I'd heard this same feedback from many different people, and over the past few years I had begun considering it myself. So I decided to write this book: "Slaughterhouse Rules." My intention in writing this book is to inspire and positively enlighten your mind, heart, and soul through the telling of my personal and professional life story. I believe that each and every one of us has enormous potential to become a better person for yourself, your family, and society. Your potential is regardless of age, race, religion, political, or financial position. Unfortunately, for many people their upward and positive potential never sees the light of day. If you are an individual who believes you're at a dead end in life, feeling stuck personally or professionally, or envisions nothing but unsurmountable barriers in front of you, then this book is for you. I also believe you will find Slaughterhouse Rules useful if you are a parent or an individual who is already successful in your professional or personal life, as we all continue to pursue our life's potential.

Slaughterhouse Rules is my story, but written for you. It's a book written about how one person worked himself out of poverty level living and destitute thinking to become a successful engineer, businessman, company leader, entrepreneur, actor, and most importantly a solid keystone for his family. This major transition had its unlikely roots while working in a slaughterhouse. This book leads you through that experience and the resulting rules I live my life by. This book is about providing you, the reader, many of my lessons learned in life. Some were learned the easy way, most the hard way. It's about triumph, success, loss, pain, and closure to life's events as a human being. I hope that when you read this book, you will internalize my life lessons for yourself then use this information to become as successful as you desire in your life and become a better person within the society in which you live. This is a book written for you, to guide you into higher level thinking while visualizing what life has to offer above and beyond what limits others may impose upon you. In a nutshell, this book is about inspiring you to become the person I believe you can become. Moreover, if I can do it, then yes, you can do it too.

Chapter 1 – The Rules

All societies have rules to live, work, or play by. There are rules that are known or perceived as regulations or governing principles. Some are dictated, whereas others are collectively agreed upon. The rules stated in this book are about those rules that I hold in resolute principle on an individual basis. I call these rules "slaughterhouse rules" because I learned and embraced these rules while working in a slaughterhouse. These principle rules became my foundation of fundamental truths that have guided, supported and helped me throughout my life's journey. The slaughterhouse rules supported me during my lowest lows and my highest highs in life. I trust that you, in turn, will embrace these rules to help you through your life's journey.

While working in the slaughterhouse, the slaughterhouse rules helped me not just survive the labor of a slaughterhouse, but also become a successful butcher workman. A butcher workman is a person who would cut, process, pack, and manage the ongoing work functions of a factory butcher. The slaughterhouse rules are:

- Accountability
- Integrity
- Resilience
- Respect
- Trust

Being *accountable* will come into play many times throughout a person's life cycle. If you're a factory worker it means showing up every day at the precise time you're required to begin work. If you're an employee that punches a clock every day then accountability states you must punch in within the defined time period, or pay the consequences. As a parent, accountability could mean acknowledging, accepting and implementing the day to day support for your family. We are all accountable for something sooner or later. Accountability also requires due diligence throughout life.

A person who demonstrates high levels of morality and ethics in their personal and work life are considered to have and uphold *integrity*. Employers seek out those individuals who are known or perceived to have integrity. As an employee of a company your actions showing truthfulness and honesty are the baseline of integrity. Individuals who show consistent integrity draw people towards them. The opposite is true with people who demonstrate a lack of integrity. Integrity is a major cornerstone to an individual's ability to succeed in his or her personal and professional lives.

Everyone has *resilience* built into their DNA. Some people are more resilient than others due to many past experiences with changes and challenges. In the workplace, people are constantly facing the challenges of organizational change. The only thing constant in life is change itself. Have you heard the phrase "When the going gets tough, the tough get going?" This phrase implies strength of character and strong internal motivation. It also implies people that have the greatest amount of resilience are better managers of stressful changes, challenges and situations. We all have varying levels of resilience; however, one can learn to heighten that level of resilience. Cumulative experiences coupled with the right attitude can strengthen your resilience and change the shape of your life's future.

Respect is engrained in the words "treat others how you want to be treated." By treating people with respect you are allowing others to respond to you in a manner you desire and expect. Respect comes in various actions such as saying thank you, not talking behind people's backs, showing empathy towards people's feelings or not insulting or making fun of someone's misfortune. Showing and giving respect toward others is inherent in the following phrase: "you catch more flies with sugar than with salt." Like resilience, the ability to treat others with respect can be learned and strengthened over the course of a lifetime.

If you are having a conversation with another person and you believe what the other person is saying, then you *trust* this person within the context of your conversation. A person you trust is a person you believe can keep secrets or private information, and doesn't lie or stretch the truth about a person or incident. If you have an inner circle of friends or family, then you most likely trust these individuals. In the workplace and in your personal life, trust is earned. When trust is broken between people it can become very difficult to trust this person again or to the degree at which they were previously trusted. Trust is a core lifetime component to becoming the best person you can be as perceived and acknowledged by others.

Thoughts for You

The purpose of the slaughterhouse rules in my life is to enable me to set meaningful life goals, resolve to stay on track, and to achieve

11

success in lifting my life from a poverty level life and way of thinking, to a life more fulfilled. The rules have helped me manage and cope with difficult losses and wonderful successes. Looking back upon my life, I learned these slaughterhouse rules provided continuity where there was significant change. Looking forward in my life, I envision the slaughterhouse rules as a solid baseline to enhance my life.

*****

"Always bear in mind that your resolution to succeed is more important than any other." Abraham Lincoln

Chapter 2 - The Formative Years

Earliest Memories

As we grow older we sometimes think back and try to remember our earliest childhood memories. These earliest memories, whether from positive or negative experiences, can have a direct impact on how we envision our future life and how we behave as adults. The earliest memory I can remember was negative when I was six years old. I got my tonsils removed and the surgery did not go well. In the early 1960's it was common medical practice to administer ether gas through a mask to place the patient into a state of unconsciousness. I remember the nurse placing a mask over my mouth and nose and being overwhelmed by the nasty smell and foul taste of vapors. Unfortunately for me, I prematurely woke up in the middle of a post-surgery emergency. Apparently the anesthetic wore off at the most inopportune time.

For decades I thought about this "incident" and couldn't figure out if it was something that actually happened to me or if it was only a bad dream. When I was in my thirties I told our mother (I had three siblings) what I remembered. I asked our mother if the picture of this incident embedded in my mind was something I dreamt or did it actually happen in real life? Our mother was very surprised that I had remembered the incident. She immediately told me about my hospital stay and the complications that ensued after having a tonsillectomy. The stitches became loose and while in the recovery room I started gagging and drowning in my own blood. Luckily, the doctor made one final checkup on his patients before heading home for the evening and found me coughing up blood. By the time I woke up, the medical team was busy saving me from knocking on death's door. I remember there was a lot of blood. Blood on my pillow, my arms and hands, all over the bed, and I had this guy (the doctor) forcing me to accept these steel rods (forceps) that were being placed down my throat. During this awakening period the doctor and nursing staff were quickly trying to stop the bleeding. Another dose of ether and I went unconscious again. The next time I woke up I remember seeing dried blood on my pillow and the bed sheets and the nurses immediately changing out my pillow and bedding. Apparently they didn't want to physically move me for fear the stitches would break loose a second time. I remember being rolled over to the recovery room where my mother and father awaited for my arrival. Our mother told me my tonsils were so big the hospital wanted to keep them and put them on display. It's unknown to me if my tonsils were placed on display but the experience made for a great school story. A positive memory of this event was during my recuperation time at home. I got to eat lots of ice cream!

I believe the reason I have remembered the hospital incident is because it was a very scary and emotional event in my life. The psychological trauma of this event made me distrust hospitals, doctors and even my parents when they took me on a doctor's visit. What is the earliest event you remember about your life? Why did you remember this event? In what ways do you believe this early childhood event, whether positive or negative, impacted you as an adolescent or an adult?

I also believe all children initially learn from their parents and family surroundings. We are all born naked, both physically and mentally. Our development is directly influenced by our parents until a future time when outside forces also influence us. For example, during my childhood years our father was a fireman so when someone asked me what I wanted to be when I grew up I always blurted out "a fireman!" On various occasions our father would take me and my three siblings to the fire station and let us climb on the bright red fire trucks and shiny metal equipment. As a very young child I could never spend enough time at our father's fire station. Having a brain like a sponge, I remember specific details of the fire station. It contained a vertical gold pole attached between the first and second floors. This "fireman's pole" allowed the firemen to slide down from the second to the first floor. The pole was located in the middle but at the rear of the station. The second floor is where the firemen would rest, sleep, eat and hang out. Just for the fun of it our father would go upstairs and slide down the pole for all of us kids to see. Visiting the fire station was a positive and rewarding experience for me during my very early childhood – from age six to about ten years old. I never turned down a time to visit the fire station. Wow, I really wanted to be a fireman! In fact, I have visited this fire station twice in my adult life. Fortunately, the building has been designated as a historical building, and all original internal and external structures depicting this building as a fire station are still in existence. Key structural items such as the fireman's pole, the emergency call-in desk, and the stairs leading up to the second floor still exist today, even though it is now repurposed as a bicycle shop.

Humans remember in pictures. Think back in your life when something impacted you as a very young child. What do you remember? Do you remember the sounds, smells, touch, or the visual context? Most likely, the picture(s) in your mind from the earliest days of your childhood are remembered like mine – in picture format. From the pictures of key events embedded in your brain, you can figure out where you were, at what age, and the event in your life that allows you to remember. Plus, you may be able to ask a parent, sibling, relative, or friend to confirm the validity of the pictures and thoughts you have stored in memory.

Children's brains are like sponges that constantly learn through new experiences. The experiences can be negative or positive in nature. You may or may not remember the day-to-day mundane life experiences. For example, you remember when your parents brought home your first puppy... and you remember when that dear pet died. They were both life impacting events; one good event and one bad event. Hence, this is what you remember the most. The vast majority of information received during puppy ownership is lost in a sea of pictured experiences that had little or no impact on your daily life. However, if the puppy chewed on the legs of your mother's prized grandfather clock and she went ballistic over it, that incident will most likely be remembered. You will probably be able to state in detail where you were, what you were doing, and why you were doing it because of the picture(s) in your mind of your mother going ballistic.

When I learned from the Brain Performance Institute that our brains do not mature until around twenty-five years of age, I understood more about my coming of age. So that's why I couldn't rent an automobile prior to turning twenty five! A lot can happen in your life from one to twenty-five years of age. Let's move on beyond my earliest memories.

Early and Solid Foundations are Key

I was lucky, very lucky, to win the lottery at such a young age. I was blessed to be born in a small Midwestern community within the United States of America. And to top it off, I got to grow up in a home with an intact family consisting of my mother, father, and three siblings. I can't imagine how difficult it would be to raise four children as a single parent – either a single mother or single father. I do know there are significant numbers of children throughout the world that come from broken or separated households. For the single parents out there, my hat goes off to you with great respect. Parenting is a tough full time job where the five slaughterhouse rules can apply day in and day out. Our family looked like the typical American Midwestern family with a solid family based foundation. I have seen and currently manage many of our past family pictures and yes, we did look like the typical American family.

Having a solid parental foundation early in life to grow as a child definitely helps to becoming successful in society. Our mother worked very hard with long hours raising four children with only six years between the eldest and the youngest. I really can't imagine how she did it. Our father the fireman was the primary wage earner. His wages placed us in the lower end of middle class America. Our mother sold

Avon products on the side to help with spending money. Any family vacations were simple and mostly centered around visiting other family members throughout the upper Midwest - Illinois, Iowa, Nebraska, and Minnesota. During our Midwest family visits we either shared rooms with cousins by sleeping on the floor or in our parents' pop-up and fold-out pull behind camper. Things were simple, compact and crowded, but it all worked.

Our home was a modest house located in a Northwestern Illinois planned community designed and built in the post WWII years. The land lots per home were about one-seventh of an acre – just big enough to support a small single family home, a one-car garage and bedrooms barely big enough for bunk beds. The local elementary school was George Washington Elementary within easy walking distance to and from the house. Both the junior and senior high schools were about one mile away. Most food shopping was done at the local A&P store located about four blocks away. All other sundry items were purchased at local strip mall stores and a few key department stores located in downtown. There were no shopping malls in those days, with many local and regional stores supporting the needs of every household. Overall, the neighborhood looked like the typical Midwestern "Ozzie and Harriet" environment. Each yard was mowed, trimmed and groomed to the expectations of the surrounding neighbors. There were sidewalks on each side of the street with large mature oak and maple trees throughout the area. As a planned community this was an ideal place to thrive as a child and grow up. We got to know all our neighbors and their children too.

During my early childhood years the family attended a local church. My siblings and I would attend Sunday school studying and learning the basics of Christianity. I also remember being baptized. Our parents showed each of us children the needed love and support to prepare for our adolescent years. Overall, this was a very good early and sound foundation for my siblings and me. I attended George Washington Elementary from kindergarten through the fourth grade. During this time period I built some close friendships with other children my age. Two of the young boys lived just a few houses away from ours. From my perspective life was all about school, sports, fun with my friends and summer time. Little did I know that as fourth grade ended, many disruptions and family moves were to replace my typical if not ideal Americana childhood.

Solid Foundations Disintegrate

Just because someone has both mother and father at home does not automatically mean everything and everyone is fine and living a wonderful life behind closed doors. Immediately after my fourth grade year we moved about three miles away into a rental property on the East side of town. We were never told why we had to move or where we were going. From this new home location my new elementary school was now Franklin Elementary which was located directly across the street from our house. I had difficulty getting to know all the new kids and felt lost in the day-to-day process of learning. Plus, I missed my friends from our old neighborhood. New kids, new school, new environment, new teachers, new everything! And yes, with every move there were bullies waiting to pounce on the new kid (me). Being an outsider to the other kids increased my fear of not being accepted, which negatively impacted my grades. I went from an A/B student to a C student. I showed interests in musical instruments such as the guitar and piano. However, any musical interests were immediately nixed by our parents due to extra costs and time.

Because of the move from one school to another, my attitude, behavior, and grades went into a downward spiral. This did not sit well with our father – who was still the primary money earner and now working longer hours that included weekends. During my fifth grade year our father grew more impatient with my behavior. From a studies perspective I was now an average to below average fifth grader. I continued to press forward with an interest in music, but my father refused to support purchasing any type of music equipment; so the opportunity of learning something related to music was again nixed. Any after school social or sporting events were also not supported. As a side note, our mother was primarily a follower and she followed our father's lead one-hundred percent. There was little emotional support and direction received from mom.

Our father became increasingly impatient with me and my siblings too.
For example, one evening after our father came home from work, he became absolutely enraged because I was late for dinner. I was late because I lost track of time while playing with a neighbor kid on his backyard trampoline. Instead of receiving a verbal reprimand and then eating dinner, he took me to the basement of the house, stripped off my

clothing, bent me over a stand-alone sawhorse and violently whipped my backside with a belt. The whipping was so bad that I couldn't sit straight in my school chair for about a week. I had raised welts, sores and deep scratches on my buttocks and behind my thighs. I wore multiple pairs of underwear to school to pad my bottom which helped me sit during class room studies. For the most part I sat on one side of my buttocks or the other. After the first week of healing I could resume normal sitting and play time with school yard friends. From the first time I was whipped by my father's belt, I began constantly to fear him.

I believe the whipping incident forever changed how our family communicated. From my perspective the punishment did not fit the crime. Depending upon the day, I couldn't figure out if our father was going to come after me for something I did wrong or didn't do within his expectations. I knew that whatever I told our mother would eventually be known by our father. I became withdrawn and feared opening up in communication with either of my parents.

Another basement whipping was in my future too. I don't remember why I was whipped the second time - maybe because of my attitude? Who knows? However, this second whipping incident wasn't as violent as the first. I suspect my father eased up on my punishment because I begged for forgiveness while being curled up in a ball on the basement floor. Regardless of the lighter whipping fare, I was absolutely terrified of my father. As a fifth grader I feared my father, was bullied in school and had below average grades with no outside supporting interests. I felt lost and empty, with no idea of what was going to happen to me from one day to the next.

After my fifth grade year our family moved again. This time we moved across town and into a newly built house which was about one-half mile from my next grade school and the adjacent junior high school. The new house was a two-story model with more space and sat on a much bigger yard. This particular house was of great interest to me because our father actually built most of it himself with some help from friends and family members. With the extra space, there was no more need for bunk beds, but sharing a bedroom with my younger brother was still required.

My next grade school was Roosevelt Elementary where I attended the sixth grade. Also, during my short stint at Roosevelt, our parents stopped taking us to church services. As children we were never told why this sudden change in our lives had occurred. The local Junior High School (Coolidge) supported the seventh and eighth grades. So, with only one year at Roosevelt I didn't have a chance to build solid friendships with other kids before being placed into the local Junior High School. Coolidge Junior High accepted students from multiple grade schools so any loosely tied friendships were difficult to maintain at this larger school. Once again I was placed into a new school with new curriculums, teachers, kids and yes – bullies.

As one can imagine I was bullied from the very beginning. I remember one particular incident where three kids were lying in wait for me after school. The main bully of the bunch immediately picked a fight with me. As luck would have it I ended up overtaking this kid, being on top and throwing down some serious punches. The next thing I knew the bully's friends jumped me and gave me a good beating. I ended up in the hospital with a bruised kidney and some other cuts and abrasions. Unfortunately for me, each time I got into a fight it turned into double jeopardy. Our father would verbally punish me and sometimes I got grounded due to fighting. For me the fighting was due to bullies and I was just trying to save myself from the obvious – a good beating from the school bully.

Over the course of two years I attended three different grade schools – Washington, Franklin, and Roosevelt. Regardless of these moves, our father expected me to either increase or maintain my grades with good studies. As a child each family move instituted new fears, uncertainties and doubts. With each new school, teachers, students, bullies, and fearing our father, my grades were average to below average.

Baseball Sustains Me

Let's back up a bit and talk about baseball. My new sixth grade school had much more to offer. They had a small baseball diamond in the back corner of the school yard. Every day at recess I tried to figure out a way to play on the baseball diamond. Of course, the diamond was off limits during recess so every time I got close to the diamond I was called by the teacher to get back up into the school yard. My favorite team was the St. Louis Cardinals. I became very engrossed into everything baseball and couldn't get my hands on enough baseball time to satisfy my over the top interest. This time our father supported me in my baseball interests and ensured I was accepted into a Little League team.

New players on a baseball team end up "riding the pine." This meant sitting on the bench and waiting for your turn to play. The coach had his favorite players within their defined positions. Luckily for me during one weekend game, things changed dramatically – no more riding the pine. Little League games have seven innings. As with any baseball league, a player could only pitch "x" number of innings within "y" number of games. For the pitchers, there was required rest between the number of innings pitched and games played. During this one particular game it was the bottom of the fifth inning with our team ahead by a few runs. The coach quickly realized he had run out of innings with the current pitcher and his other previous pitchers were still inside their resting periods. The coach turned to the bench and yelled out "any of you guys know how to pitch?" I raised my hand and said "Yes, I can pitch." What the coach didn't know was that I had been practicing pitching baseballs in our backyard. During my practice sessions my brother refused to catch for me because I threw the ball too hard and fast for him to catch. Our father would catch for me on occasions and was surprised at my ability to throw powerful strikes. While practicing pitching, I would throw baseballs into a makeshift wooden back stop that sported a defined strike zone. Back at the baseball game I was selected to relieve the exhausted pitcher and with fierce attitude, started throwing strikes. I struck out all remaining batters throughout the rest of the game. From that time forward I became one of the starting pitchers for our baseball team.

During my two-year tenure as a Little League player I would become the pitcher that other teams feared. I also earned a position on the All Star team across two consecutive years. From a baseball perspective everything was going great! I am now in Middle School which consisted of grades seven and eight. My baseball pitching prowess was on the rise. I now had a fast ball, slider and sinker. With the ability to throw three different pitches I became a local hot commodity for the Babe Ruth League teams. With Little League behind me I quickly signed up for a local Babe Ruth team. These teams consisted of players too old to play Little League but too young to play in the Minor Leagues. I quickly became the youngest starting pitcher on my new Babe Ruth team. My school grades pulled up to average and my baseball expertise was outstanding. Life was good and I had plans that included lots of baseball.

Thoughts for You

It's up to you to manage your early childhood experiences – either good or bad. Bad things seem to happen very quickly, whereas the good things in life take time to bear fruit. Do you want to dwell on the bad experiences or the good experiences? The choice is yours; one that only you can make and decide. I believe you should trust yourself first. I chose to focus my early childhood memories on being an outstanding baseball player. Those thought pictures in your mind from your early childhood years are most likely the very early truths of your life. View the bad pictures as what they are and nothing more. Do your best not to dwell on negative thought pictures from your earliest childhood memories. Bring forward the positive impacting thoughts that got you where you are today. Be thankful you have positive early childhood pictures in your mind and leverage these thoughts to bring a smile to your face.

Constant moving between public schools is difficult for any child to endure. I didn't fare well with my grade school moves and my grades showed it. Plus, I felt there was little support from our father and very minimal understanding of why we were moving around as a family. If the family must move I believe each child inside the family should be given a voice to be heard about their fears, misunderstandings and expectations. Moving can be a positive experience if managed correctly. Unfortunately for our family, each move increased fears and non-communication that had negative impacts on school grades and social acceptance. It wasn't until later in my life that I could move forward and beyond their impactful effects.

*****

"We must let go of the life we have planned, so as to accept the one that is waiting for us." Joseph Campbell

Chapter 3 - Pushed to the Farm

A Reality Shift

During the middle school years our father was busy with other work outside of town. It seemed as though all our father's weekends were filled with work on a piece of property about fifteen miles east of our current home. Whereas I thought weekends during the summer months were for baseball, our father thought otherwise. Instead of planning for a weekend of baseball and/or family outings, I found my brother and I being hauled out to a country property that was mixed use between tillable soil and a timber area. Abruptly, and with no explanation, our father told us that he had purchased the land and it needed some work. The work consisted of clearing out old dead trees and brush. My brother (one year younger than myself) and I ended up spending many weekends working the new property – a very long way from playing any baseball and building new friendships.

One workday evening our father came home from work and again started talking about spending the weekend at the property. My mind was set on pitching a baseball game Saturday afternoon. I began complaining about missing baseball games and not wanting to spend the weekend working at the property. Our father became enraged with my disposition and decided a good whipping would alter or change my mind. This time he came after me with his belt and fists. After a short bout of whipping with complete chaos, I was subdued into accepting the inevitable. From that point forward I stopped complaining about not playing baseball and withdrew openly communicating things that bothered me. I quickly learned that I couldn't turn to our mother for help or a consoling heart. It turned out our mother was a very good follower to our father. I never again stepped foot onto a baseball field, nor did I ever play baseball again.

Fear, Anger and Loss

The mixed use farm land our father purchased was directly connected to that of a local farmer. This farmer was a friend of our father's and owned approximately 800 acres of tillable land across two different farms. There were many barns, stables, and other buildings that housed horses, chickens, pigs and cattle. The tillable land was used for planting corn and/or soy beans. The first day our father drove me and my brother out to his friend's farm he dropped us off to "work the barns." My brother and I had never been inside a barn nor had we ever worked on a real working farm. As I stood in front of this massive barn filled with horses residing in their stalls, a huge mountain of a man stepped outside and began barking orders of all the work that needed to be accomplished. I quickly learned our father had given his farmer friend full authority to put us to work and provide punishment to my brother and myself as needed. I immediately feared this man as he was much larger than our father and had an even larger no nonsense attitude. This farmer also had sons of his own and they were already working inside the barn. Luckily for me his oldest son was my age and knew a lot about cleaning out horse stalls and barns. He ended up teaching me everything I needed to know about working the barns.

The very last thing I wanted to do in life was work on a farm and clean a horse barn. I had no idea why I had to perform this work. I felt lost, confused, frustrated, and angered about what was happening to my life. I was given no explanations by either of my parents and there were no discussions about why I had to clean barns or what the immediate future looked like as a thirteen year old boy. I felt deep anger towards our father and resented being treated as a farmhand child slave. During this time period, our father created a few new nicknames for me such as *Dummy, Worthless* and *Stupid*. Depending upon the day and type of work being performed our father would yell out to me with statements like "Hey Dummy," or "What are you doing Worthless?" To my embarrassment, he had the knack of saying these things to me while in front of the other farm boys. He was also quick to say "You do good work but not enough of it." As one can imagine this type of verbal abuse along with the fear of being whipped depleted my sense of self-worth and dignity. My younger brother stood along the sidelines watching our father treat me maliciously, then at a later time, would launch complaints to me privately – most likely for self-preservation. He knew the punishment was harsh if he complained to our father or slacked on his work ethic.

I was more vocal about the dirty and dangerous work we had to do throughout the summer. However, as each day of the early summer passed I internalized the acceptance of our new reality. Little did I know that this was not just a summertime gig, but was the beginning of an entirely new lifestyle for me and our family. During the summer months our father sold our home in the city and we moved onto a farm located about six miles away from the nearest small town. The town had about sixty-five hundred residents and primarily supported the local rural farming industry. The farm where our family lived had old buildings including the farm house. The farm house was old, dirty and in need of repair. It was a two story structure with a dirt floor basement. The heating system ran from an outdoor propane tank. There was no air conditioning and all windows were single pane glass that constantly leaked. The plumbing and electrical system was very sub-standard. Our work assignments included sealing windows, painting, clearing weeds, general cleaning, and performing any maintenance to ensure habitability. This included trapping and killing any vermin that built nests inside and around the house. To help with keeping the house insulated, we stacked hay bales around the outside lower perimeter of the house. During the summer months the house was always too hot and humid, during the winter months – too cold. The newly occupied farm house was a much harsher living environment, plus we were isolated out in the country. It felt like we had lost a standard of living the family was accustomed too.

Hard Work, Sweat, and Little Pay

The summer turned out to be dirty and hot, with long hours working two different farms. Between the two farms the livestock count was approximately three hundred fifty steers, two hundred fifty pigs, three hundred chickens, and seventy horses. I quickly learned that all livestock needed to be fed every morning and night regardless of weather or holidays. There were chores to perform every day of the week. The two farms were about one to two miles apart and accessible via tractor roads carved out of the earth between fields. Working real farms with livestock is dangerous work. We were told to be careful around the pig pens because if you fell in, the pigs would attack and tear you apart. Tractors and their implements were constantly in motion. We wore hard hats, work gloves and knee high boots when cleaning out stalls, barns and sheds. Depending upon the type of livestock there was a constant smell of manure which intensified as the summer heat increased. The chicken coop was the worst. When we cleaned the chicken coop the manure smell was so intense it was like walking into an ammonia cloud. It would practically take your breath away. While inside the chicken coop, we constantly had to guard our back sides because the roosters would attack and spur us with their front claws.

Every Saturday was spent cleaning out the barns and loafing sheds, mowing weeds, fixing fences, painting farming structures, washing trucks and tractors and digging drainage ditches. Every Sunday morning was no longer church time. Our Sunday mornings were filled with cleaning horse stalls and collecting chicken eggs from the hens in the chicken coop. Our free time to play as children was awarded after the horse barn was clean, chicken eggs collected and all other daily chores (feeding all the livestock) finished.

One of the main structures on the farm was an old eighty feet tall by forty feet wide concrete silo. The silo stored corn silage that was used to feed the cattle. Unfortunately, this particular silo did not have any automated systems to move and distribute the corn silage that fed the cattle out in the feed lot. Corn silage stored in enclosed silos without proper ventilation builds methane gas which is highly explosive and toxic to breath. The silo was vented at the top which allowed the corn silage to eliminate its methane gas and dry out over time. My brother and I waited until it was deemed safe by our father before manually working the silo to feed the cattle. For protection we wore dust masks but had nothing to protect us from any pockets of methane gas. While my brother hated working the silo I supported him the best I could and together we made the best of it. Once given the green light we used pitch forks and scoop shovels with a wheelbarrow to feed the cattle. This meant someone had to climb up the inside door ladder attached to the silo until you reached the top of the corn silage. From there, the silage was pitched down the ladder shoot to an awaiting wheel barrow. With each wheel barrow full of corn silage the person managing the wheel barrow would walk the silage out to the end of the feed line where the silage was dumped for the cattle to eat. This process continued every day, twice a day until the silo was empty (about one year). My brother and I took turns managing the wheel barrow and pitching corn silage. The silo work was added to our already busy daily chores and seemed never ending.

Summer was over and school was back in session. This meant getting up early enough to ensure the chores were accomplished while allowing time to shower, eat breakfast and prepare for school. After school the chores had to be finished prior to dinner. The chores had to be done regardless of any extra-curricular activities offered by the school. The entire experience was hard work, lots of sweat with many new learning curves to tackle. As a rookie farm boy I was paid twenty-five cents an hour. This pittance of pay didn't begin to cover the amount of

32

hard work and sweat equity I put into working the two farms. I felt like a child laborer living in the moment with very little view into the future. I was living in another world that seemed very distant to playing baseball and dreaming of entering the minor leagues.

Work Ethic, Traits and Skills

There were some good behavioral traits and skills I learned while living the farm life. What I didn't know then was that these new traits and skills would support me as an adult for many years to come. For example, I learned how to fix just about anything with available tools or build something with minimal resources. My new work ethic and level of diligence had become very strong. On a daily basis I found myself working towards earning some free time. Our free time was spent with the other farm boys learning how to create our own fun. Fun on the farm included working on trucks, tractors, swimming in the local pond or riding horses. Once in a while we threw in a few wrestling matches between us boys.

While living on the farm I also learned how to hunt and fish on our own property and the adjoining properties of other farmers. Since our father was a hunter and fisherman himself, I had already learned the skills needed to safely manage shot guns for small game and fishing the local lakes, rivers and streams. We learned to hunt and fish only during licensed seasons and bring home to the dinner table whatever we caught or killed.

By the end of my fourteenth year I was driving pickup trucks, small to large sized tractors, hunting on my own and becoming a very accountable adolescent. I was operating tractors while pulling and manipulating implements such as discs, plows and other farming equipment. I will always remember the day when I was allowed to go hunting on my own. That was the day I knew I was becoming a real man.

A New School

My freshman year in high school consisted of making new friends and being teased and beaten by a couple school bullies. The local high school was small and supported various cliques of students. I quickly learned that the majority of the students had known each other since kindergarten, played football together throughout all their years of school, and had very little patience or support for newcomers. Also, the school had no baseball team of any kind. Our father insisted that I play football instead, because this was the main sport supported by the high school and across this small farming community. I had never played football nor did I know anything about the game. For me, freshman football practices were filled with fear, uncertainty, doubt, and a growing hatred for everything football. I remained resistant to playing football until one day my father told me unconditionally that I was going to play football, or else. I relented and immersed myself into the sport. I was disappointed that my father never showed up at a practice and attended only one football game throughout my freshman and sophomore years of school.

I received little support from our father when playing the game of football. I remember thinking to myself that if this was my new reality, then I would need to be stronger physically. So I asked my father

34

to buy me a weight set so I could build up my body and compete with and against these big, tough farm boys. About midway through my freshman year, my father obliged, and I started pumping iron with my new one-hundred-ten pound weight set. For example, our primary fullback for the varsity team was a sophomore weighing in at two hundred twenty pounds and six feet two inches tall. It always took at least two defensive players to tackle him. Believe me, many of these farm boys meant business on the football field. I also competed in track & field (mostly running the eight-eighty and competing in cross country races), worked my ass off on the farms, and became a pretty decent football player.

With dedication to my studies and hard work to my weight set, my grades improved to a B average and I began to build muscles needed to succeed in football. By my mid-sophomore year, I also had a full time girlfriend – a petite little blond girl that I was becoming crazy about. I discovered that I excelled in wood shop, metal shop and mechanical drawing. I learned I was very good at detailed and specific tasks, such as mechanical drawing, and I began thinking I wanted to be an architect. I enjoyed the precision instruments of the drawing table and the freedom to create an architectural drawing from an idea. This roller coaster of my early life was looking up for me – farm life, football, good grades, girlfriend, and other farm friends with whom I truly enjoyed sharing my time.

Two More Bad Moves

It was now late in my sophomore year of high school and everything on the farm appeared to be in place and moving along as expected. Summer was just around the corner and I was looking forward to having a school break. Our father was now working as a job foreman at a local caisson company. The company was owned by our father's farmer friend. One day in mid-summer our father came home and announced that we were moving to Nebraska. The family was shocked beyond belief as our father was the only one who desired to move. Apparently, our father negotiated a deal with his older brother and became partner in a new start-up company. He was bull headed and determined that his new business venture would be the best thing ever with him making millions of dollars. The new venture was in the pickup truck camper trailer business. Our father and his brother created an automated system that mounted and dis-mounted pickup truck campers from the truck. The intent was to sell this new solution throughout all the Recreational Vehicle (RV) shows throughout the country. Our father was to be a Vice President in the company and charge forward with all sales and marketing aspects of the business. Regardless of how much the family complained and raised issues with moving, our father marched forward with moving plans. By the end of the summer we were on the road and moving to a small town in Eastern Nebraska (about twenty miles West of Omaha).

Unfortunately for me and my siblings, this Nebraska farm town was very small with only about one-thousand two-hundred inhabitants. The high school was tiny and not a true high school. It was a junior-senior high school that supported grades seven through twelve. The available high school curriculum was sub-standard to the extent that I ended up taking wood shop, mechanical drawing and a math class over again because there was nothing else to take. The school district had little money with very minimal support for extra-curricular activities. The school was built for air conditioning with each classroom having a single window. However, the district ran out of money and put the purchase of air conditioning units on hold. During the spring and early summer months, the class rooms would get so hot and humid the teachers would refuse to teach. Multiple times classes were taught outdoors with students sitting in an adjacent grassy field.

As usual, there were school bullies lying in wait and ready to pounce on any new kid(s). My strategy to keep away from the bullies was to spend as much time as I could in the school library. My strategy didn't work as I got myself excused from school for three days because I got into a fight in the school library! There was no place to hide from the bullies nor were there any advanced academic courses to take that interested me. Just as before, there was double jeopardy when getting into a fight – a bad situation in school and at home.

The farm house we moved into in Eastern Nebraska was in the same poor condition as the farm house in Illinois. Again, we had to perform many repairs to ensure the house was habitable. There was no air conditioning and the heating system was a piece of junk. Everything seemed to either leak, fall apart or needed repair. We moved from one worn out farm house to another.

I was heartbroken over leaving my girlfriend and truly missed the friendships I had created with other farm boys back home. My grades plummeted to the C/D range, and my attitude was filled with anger, rage and resentment. I started growing my hair long and hanging out with the less than desirable young men. Within this new group of young men, drugs and alcohol were common fare. Our father kept up with the name calling and added a new nick name to the list - calling me "Hip." This was short for hippie. What he didn't realize was that I was rebelling against everything he represented and was eager to leave behind a family wrought with verbal and physical abuse. I was so engrossed in saving myself from our father's verbal and physical abuse that I lost the basics of communication with my siblings. I guess each of us was doing our own thing and moving in different directions. Prior to my senior graduation my older sister became pregnant, got married and moved out of the house. Our younger sister would disappear from the house for days only to return with a new boyfriend. My younger brother kept to himself and did his best not to rock the boat – his standard self-preservation behavior. From my perspective, our family was in ruins.

I was working for my uncle's construction company doing small jobs on weekends. Many instances I would call in sick from school on Friday's so I could travel with the job crew to other mid-western towns and earn a five dollar an hour wage. You may recall I was making twenty five cents an hour back on the Illinois farm, so five dollars an hour at a part-time job was big money for me. As an ex-farm boy with a strong work ethic, I was in high demand with the construction foremen.

The construction foremen would argue between themselves who would get me on their weekend work teams.

The reality of the situation was that our family was falling apart from the inside out and hanging on by a thread. My three siblings seemed to be doing their own thing in life. Our mother was under significant stress because our father was constantly on the road selling and positioning his new camper trailer solution. The family situation was bleak and so was my school performance. With near failing grades, I barely graduated from high school. I did however manage to graduate – perhaps because the principal just wanted to get rid of me! From my perspective the overall value and quality of the education I had received was below average to poor. I attribute this to the constant moving and lack of communication and support received inside the family. Late in my senior year of high school our father's business venture fell apart. Again, our father came home and announced that we were moving back to our original farm town in Illinois at the end of the summer. It was time for the next phase of my life: new beginnings, lost roads and a strong will to survive.

Thoughts for You

As a seventeen year old filled with anger, rage, frustration and little sense of purpose or direction, I had no idea what I was going to do with my life. However, I did own a very strong work ethic and within myself I knew I was honest, trustworthy, and hard working. These three learned traits, coupled with the energy of youth and a bit of street smarts, would help me survive future life experiences. No matter how bad things would become, deep within me I knew that I was a good person from the inside out, and that things would work out for the better.

Think about the key learned traits you now have or had as a young person or adult. Did you leverage these supporting traits to move yourself forward and create a better life for yourself and/or your family? I believe that everyone has something to positively offer in life. The traits I learned from farm life allowed me to believe I had something much better to offer in life. Yes, you may currently be young in age and not fully realize your potential (just like I was), but as your life progresses you will find a way to better yourself and the world around you. The longer you live and learn, the more opportunity you have to understand and believe in your own upward mobility. Keep focused on the future, don't live in your negative past, forgive those who have trespassed or wronged you and things will work out better than you expect.

*****

"When I let go of what I am, I become what I might be." Lao Tzu

Chapter 4 - The Never Ending Search

Transition Jobs and a Friend

Our father's strained relationship with his brother eliminated my part-time five dollar an hour job. Fresh out of high school at the young age of seventeen, the first order of business was to find a full time summer job in the local area. This meant any job that would pay me enough money to save back until I could manage to live on my own. A friend of mine from high school introduced me to a local bricklayer who pointed me to a friend of his who owned a rock wall terracing company. The company built rock walls for terracing along roadways, buildings, driveways and just about any place supporting rock walls were needed. The pay was two dollars seventy-five cents an hour. The work was back breaking, sweaty, and dirty with ten to twelve hour work days, six days a week, and no insurance. All day long I would shovel dirt, pick up, carry, and place rocks in pre-defined places. I worked at this rock wall company over the hot summer months until my father pulled together his plan to move back to northwest Illinois.

My father asked me to help with the packing and, of course, the actual moving. I was not a quitter, nor do I ever fail to show up for work without a valid cause. Knowing we were moving back to Illinois, I was relieved to move on from the rock wall terracing company. Between the previous part-time construction job during my high school days and the full time position at the rock wall terracing company, I managed to save enough money to purchase an older model pick-up truck. We packed my truck full of household goods and, along with the other household items and vehicles, we caravanned ourselves back to Illinois. Upon our return to the small farm town, our father purchased a modest four bedroom home in town. I was given my own upstairs bedroom with attached outside stairs that gave me access to the side yard of the house. This outside staircase would prove instrumental in my future plans.

My mental state was still one of anger, rage and frustration. I felt I was without a sense of purpose, or direction and having no idea what I was going to do with my life. My father kept pressuring me to "get a job, boy." Finding half-way decent and available full time work in a small farm town is not an easy task. Most of the full time jobs were either low paying retail positions in town or as a farm hand for local farmers. You have to know people and network your way around to find the good jobs. I didn't know anyone, as the majority of people I previously knew in high school were either off to college or I didn't know where to find them. I started frequenting a couple of the local taverns after working hours as this was their busiest time of each work day. From one of the local taverns I managed to connect with a couple of old school friends who still lived in the area. The job news was not great. My school friends told me that decent paying jobs in the local area were very difficult to obtain.

Striking Out On My Own

My father was constantly pressuring me to find work and belittling me on a daily basis with his abusive nicknames. Finally, I scripted an action plan to escape town and strike out on my own. I calculated that if I used my truck for traveling I could be found by either

42

local or state authorities. As a legal minor I safely assumed my parents would actively search for my whereabouts. So, staying on foot was part of the plan. I convinced a local friend to pick me up early one weekday morning just as the sun was coming up – around 6:00 a.m. This same friend was also willing to store my pickup truck on his property until my return at a future date. I figured I would be back before winter and prior to the real cold gripping the area. One night I secretly packed a duffle bag with needed clothing and some foul weather gear. With one hundred dollars cash in my wallet, I quietly made my way down the outside staircase and out to a local street corner where I waited for my friend to pick me up. As planned, my friend picked me up on his way to work, drove me out to Interstate 80 (about five miles away) and dropped me off alongside the road.

I began hitchhiking my way west. For the most part I was being picked up by semi-truck drivers with an occasional single driver in a car or pickup truck. Each of them would ask me, "Where you headed?" and my answer was "West." I ended up in central Wyoming! Unfortunately for me it took about two weeks to get to central Wyoming. This was due to poor choices of rides coupled with being dropped off on lonely and lightly traveled country highways.

For the first time in my life I was living homeless. I felt free and out from under the constant verbal abuse of my father. Luckily, on the farm I spent a lot of time outdoors in the elements and I also knew how to camp outside in all forms of foul weather. Even though I was living outdoors alone and homeless, I had the basic skills and knowledge to survive outdoors in the elements. I was not one hundred percent broke, as I did have a small amount of cash just in case of emergencies. It was the summer months, so I didn't have to worry about long, cold, freezing nights. I could have stayed in Wyoming and found work, but I knew my older sister lived in South Dakota. From central Wyoming I decided to start hitch hiking my way east to South Dakota.

Standing alongside a Wyoming county highway a trucker stopped and picked me up. This guy had a small container of white pills in the counsel of his tractor truck located between our seats. About once an hour he would pop a pill and ask me if I wanted one. Knowing it was some form of amphetamine, I said "thanks but no thanks." Wherever the destination, this trucker was definitely going to get there on time or early. During our travels together he was required to stop at a weigh station and as luck would have it, his rig was over the weight limit. He was hauling soy beans and asked me if I was willing to shovel soy beans from one truck to another for a small payment. I told him that I had not eaten a decent meal for over three days and felt too weak to shovel beans. The trucker agreed to buy me a hot meal at the adjoining truck stop in trade for shoveling beans – a trade which I gladly accepted. I managed to shovel enough beans out of his truck to pass within the weight limit. Back on the road we then headed east toward Rapid City, South Dakota.

From the time I left home until I ended up at my sister's home in South Dakota the total time living out on the road was three weeks. During these travels I was living under highway overpasses, alongside highway culvert systems and just about anywhere I could find adequate shelter. Due to my very tight budget, I committed myself to knocking on the back door of churches to ask for a food handout. Each church I stumbled upon gave me either a warm meal or drove me to a local diner or fast food restaurant and purchased a meal of my choice. I learned a true sense of humility, and was always very grateful, humble, and thankful for their help. These were true acts of kindness that I never forgot, that's for sure.

Reservation Living

My final destination turned out to be about two and one-half hours southeast of Rapid City, South Dakota. My older sister lived in the small town called Martin and I figured this was a good place to land. Martin is about forty miles east of Wounded Knee. From a historical perspective the entire area around Wounded Knee in 1973 was a volatile and somewhat dangerous place. If you were not identified as a Native American Indian, people had the tendency to harass and possibly take a couple pot shots at you with whatever gun was available. The volatility of the region was created because the American Indian Movement (AIM) seized control of Wounded Knee to protest and then to demand the impeachment of tribal president Richard Wilson, who they accused of corruption and abuse of political opponents. Inclusive with the seizing of Wounded Knee, protesters also targeted the United States government's failure to fulfill treaties with Native American Indians and demanded the reopening of treaty negotiations. I was fascinated to learn about the uprising and why the Native American Indians stood up for an honorable cause.

Having successfully thumbed my way to my sister's house, she and her husband (a professional golfer) allowed me to stay in their trailer home with one exception, I had to sleep on the floor. During my short tenure at my sister's trailer home she contacted our parents to let them know I was alive and doing OK. In the interim I found work driving a tractor and tilling wheat fields for a local rancher. The wheat fields of South Dakota seemed to go on forever. The work was boring, lonely, dirty and paid two dollars an hour which included three meals a day and the use of a second hand ranch truck. I quickly learned that as a Caucasian Midwestern farm boy driving around the Pine Ridge Reservation countryside I was a prime shooting target. I worried about sitting on a lone tractor out in the middle of nowhere. I asked my rancher employer for use of a shot gun or rifle for self-protection. He gave me both. When driving between the ranch and town I always drove as fast as I could and did my best to stay on the main roads. It was a crazy and dangerous place and time.

I was given instructions to have "X" acres of fields tilled in "Y" amount of time. Having a strong work ethic and upholding my own accountability helped me to finish many of the field tilling jobs early. On the weekends and sometimes during the week after tilling the fields, I would work part-time at the local golf course as a repairman/laborer. I worked on golf carts, mowed grass, kept the local grounds clean, and learned to tear down and build golf course T-boxes and putting greens. I enjoyed the golf course work as it was something new and different from farming, and the labor component was much easier and cleaner. Most golf courses and local land establishments in the area had gopher problems. Certain areas of the golf course were riddled with gopher holes and caused huge property problems. Gopher management was achieved by one person driving the golf cart while the other person shot at gophers with a shot gun. One area of the course needed significant repairs. A decision was made to acquire some explosives (small sticks of dynamite) blast out the area, thereby relieving ourselves of gophers while making the earth easy to manipulate with a shovel. The process worked quite effectively. Remembering how we managed the gopher population, it probably looked like a Hollywood scene cut from the movie Caddy Shack! I also made friends with some of the local country club members, who would occasionally buy me a beer or offer up a very nice meal. As a little side bonus I learned to play golf with the local club professional (my brother-in-law). In just a few months I was posting scores in the eighties which I assumed everyone who played the game was doing. Gosh, if I could just do that consistently today!

First Glimpse of College

With winter just around the corner, my tenure at Martin and the Pine Ridge Reservation was coming to an end. I decided to hitchhike myself back to Omaha and reconnect with some friends. However, this time I stayed on the main interstate system to catch rides. By staying on the main interstate system, I didn't have to worry about getting dropped off out in the middle of nowhere on a lonely stretch of country road. My brother-in-law was heading back to Rapid City for golf course supplies and gave me a ride to Interstate 90. From there I hitchhiked a ride east and somehow ended up in Brookings, South Dakota. Truckers have a way of driving to their destinations with a strong focus, hence showing up in Brookings. Brookings is the home of South Dakota State University. I really liked the college town activities and nightlife, so I decided to stick around for about a month. I found an interim place to live (a temporary boarding house) and got a job as a ditch digger for a local telecommunications company. One day while on the job at the college campus I was on break talking to a local student and asked him about college life, courses to take and just about anything else he was willing to share. He showed me his class schedule and openly invited me to his late evening English class located on the campus grounds. The next thing I knew, I was sitting in a large class room of college students listening to a professor talk about the conventions of the English language. I was definitely a fish out of water and had no idea about what to do, how to do it, or where to go. As expected, my English classroom time was very short lived. I was in Brookings for just a few weeks when it came time for me to head south and locate my friends in eastern Nebraska (Omaha). My goal was to make it back to Illinois before the nasty winter weather gripped the region.

Re-Connecting With Friends

Back on the road I hitchhiked rides South on Interstate 29, which took me to Omaha, Nebraska. From there I managed to reconnect with a couple high school friends. I found temporary living quarters in a friend's apartment while once again sleeping on the floor in my sleeping bag. My friend was currently working for a local construction company and managed to get me hired as a laborer. This particular company built

48

large single and sometimes multi-story metal buildings. My job was to install large bolts, nuts and washers where the upper ceiling girder system connected itself to the super structure. This meant balancing and walking along the tops of girders from twenty to sixty feet off the ground while being weighed down around my waist with thirty pounds of bolts, nuts and washers. In the early morning hours the girders were cold, wet and slippery. One minor misstep and you would be lucky to end up in the hospital. What I didn't realize at the time was that this job would be a precursor to my future employment that entailed working heights.

It was getting to be late fall and the cold was setting in for any outdoor work. The steel metal building job lasted about one month. I earned just enough money to ensure I wasn't penniless during my trip back to Illinois. I decided to leave Omaha but planned to return within a couple of weeks. One of my high school friends drove me out to Interstate 80 and dropped me off. I was back on the road thumbing myself east to my home location in northwest Illinois. Upon my return I had one hundred dollars in my wallet – the same amount as I left with months prior.

Showing up at my parent's house was an interesting moment in time. For the first time in my life my father was somewhat calm about our relationship and my mother followed his lead. I was allowed to move back into my room upstairs with the expectation of paying rent. The "Get a job, boy" statement from my father showed its ugly face again. I mentioned to both my parents that inside a two week period I would be collecting all my personal items, loading up my pickup truck and heading back to Omaha. I was told unceremoniously that as a minor I was not allowed to leave and live on my own until I turned eighteen. Nevertheless within two weeks I was definitely out the door and driving myself back to Omaha.

While in Omaha I connected with my friends again and started discussing job options. I told them about my tenure as a part-time construction laborer during my high school days. My role as a construction laborer was to help the carpenters move equipment around and keep the job site clean. As a part-time construction laborer with a strong work ethic I made a good impression with the head carpenters. You may recall in the previous chapter I stated that head carpenters would argue about who was going to get me as their work mate during short weekend jobs. I made a couple of phone calls into my uncle's construction company and was immediately hired as a full-time employee working as a construction laborer. Apparently, the disagreements between my uncle and my father had resided. However, the first available work was located in the State of Texas.

Professional Construction

The construction company I was working for out of Omaha had multiple jobs in multiple states. The company specialized in very large commercial insulation projects. I was assigned to a non-union job site in the panhandle of Texas. This particular work site was located about fifteen miles north of Dumas, TX in a location called Cactus. The job site consisted of building a huge beef kill packing plant. Insulating this facility would take upwards of two full years. I arrived six months into

50

the insulation project. Our job was to insulate all walls, floors, roofs, pipes, joists and ceilings in every room across the job site. The largest of the main buildings was a cold storage structure standing one hundred ten feet tall. To insulate the walls and upper ceiling joints a scaffold was required to be built from floor to ceiling. It took thousands of pounds of scaffolding to cover twenty five percent of one wall. The scaffolding was so large and heavy, we had to dismantle fifty percent of the structure and move it via an electric winch. Each time we had to move the scaffolding it took three days of work. We had to build it up, tear it down, build it up and tear it down. Finalizing the insulation of one inside wall was a major accomplishment. Since I had already worked heights in my earlier steel building job in Nebraska these new heights were not a barrier for me to overcome. I learned very quickly to respect heights and always live by "safety first." This meant taking my time, doing the job right the first time, and trusting the integrity of the work accomplished. Our head carpenter's foreman had a favorite saying *"Off your ass, on your feet, out of the shade and into the heat - get back to work."* I heard this at least once every day. Yes, this man demanded respect for his position and held you accountable for all your work. Whatever job this man told me to do, I ensured it got done (lest get my butt kicked all over the job site). This type of work didn't wear on me negatively. I was now making five dollars an hour with health insurance, which was a step up from the menial labor jobs I had been performing over the many months while living on the road.

A "Friend"

Life in the panhandle was OK, but nothing to write home about. I spent my free time either riding dirt bikes, rattlesnake hunting, or drinking at the local pubs in Dumas, Dalhart or Pampa, then getting into fights with the local cowboys. I became very good at billiards, foosball, and fisticuffs. My foosball expertise was good enough to get me into small local tournaments where I could harass and give the local cowboys a hard time. I guess there was not much else to do in the panhandle.

I did, however, have my own single furnished bedroom apartment and my own transportation. My personal integrity was in good order and my resilience to overcome obstacles had shown its positive side. There was no more living under overpasses or in drainage ditches and no more asking for handouts from local churches. I was maintaining enough bank balance to offer me a small cushion to live on just in case of emergencies. In spite of working myself into a better paying job, I was still lost within myself and searching for something better. I didn't mind working hard, but I didn't see where any of my hard work was going to take me in life.

I was pursuing a young woman who worked part time at the local grocery store. We would go to the occasional movie or just hang out and meet up with local friends. One evening she invited me over to her parent's house for dinner. Upon meeting her father I learned he was the local chief of police. With my long hair and being an outsider, her father quickly dismissed me and privately told me not to pursue his daughter. Being eighteen, ignorant, and bull headed, I ignored her father's warning and maintained my pursuit of his daughter. Her father really didn't like

me and decided to show his force. At every opportunity he would follow me around town in his police car and pull me over for any small or perceived traffic infraction. His harassment continued for many weeks. His disdain for me continued to the point where I defaulted to riding my bicycle when going out and around town. He even resorted to following me while on my bicycle and pulled me over multiple times for ridiculous minimal infractions. I finally relented and agreed to not pursue his daughter.

During an early weekday evening I heard a knock on my apartment door to find my ex-girlfriend's father and another policeman wanting to talk with me about stealing merchandise from a local department store. I defended myself and told them I didn't steal anything and they were talking to the wrong man. I noticed in the back seat of the police car an acquaintance "friend" of mine. He apparently told them a story about how the two of us broke into the department store and stole various articles of clothing and whatever else we could load into my pickup truck. None of this ever happened. I strongly suspected this young man was the true thief and to save himself he'd cut a deal with my ex-girlfriend's father. The next day the police showed up with a warrant to search my apartment. If I couldn't produce a receipt or legal document for possessing any of my personal clothing items, furniture, stereo, or kitchen appliances, they were considered stolen. I was taken in custody and arrested for receiving stolen merchandise. With very little money and no outside legal assistance I was dependent on the legal system to run its course. I spent three weeks in the county jail awaiting arraignment on the bogus charges. Finally, a court appointed attorney was assigned to my case and I got to appear before the judge. The attorney told me if I didn't plead guilty to a misdemeanor I would be back in the county jail. The misdemeanor required a one year "Stay out of trouble" probation period and a five hundred dollar fine. Not wanting to spend any more time in jail, I relented to the charge, signed the applicable documents, and was immediately released.

Upon my release I was told to stop by the police station to pick up personal belongings and obtain my pickup truck from the police impound lot. All that was left of my personal belongings was a small bag of clothing; furthermore, I had to pay a fee to get my truck out of the police department's impound lot. After spending three weeks in the county jail I lost access to my apartment. Hence, I was back out on the street with no place to live and uncertain if I still had a construction job. I spent the next week living out of my truck and getting my job back. I was successful on the job front and quickly began earning a living again. I also found another apartment to rent. Within a few weeks I learned from other local friends that most of my furniture was given away and my stereo system ended up in my ex-girlfriend's bedroom. I felt and believed that justice was abused, and that I was profiled and used as a pawn to self-serve other's egos and power hungry appetites. However, I believed deep down that my personal integrity and strong work ethic were still intact.

Moving On

After one year working in the Texas Panhandle I received a phone call from the construction company's home office telling me to report to another job site – this one was located in Fort Morgan, Colorado, seventy five miles northeast of Denver. This job site, like the one in Cactus, Texas was a non-union site. As a full time employee with the company and having no union card, I was restricted to non-union job sites. Needless to say, I was eager to move out of Texas and onto a new and better opportunity. Within three working days I was in Fort Morgan reporting to another site foreman. This man was very hard working and didn't take no for an answer from anyone. With experience in working heights plus a solid work record, I assumed the company thought it a smart move for me to be in Fort Morgan. This construction site offered working heights exceeding one hundred-twenty feet.

Upon arrival I quickly learned that I was promoted to carpenter's apprentice. I got to start using my brain as much as my body to get things done. My primary job was to make all the carpentry cuts as directed by the carpenters. The carpenters would be up on the scaffolding, yell down what type of product and cut was needed and I would make it happen. I was also put in charge of all the on-site laborers which meant I got to babysit adult men and ensure they did their labor jobs. Most laborers were easy to manage but there were always those individuals that spent more time trying to figure out how not to work instead of just getting the job done. I soon learned that babysitting grown men all day long on a commercial job site was not very enjoyable. I did not complain about the new assignment and decided to make the most of it. Besides this was more of a leadership position and I wanted to show everyone I had the moxie to do the job.

From Fort Morgan you could see the Rocky Mountains on clear days. The mountains had a luring effect on me so I decided to spend some available weekends pitching a tent somewhere in the Rockies. My target area for camping was Rocky Mountain National Park located just outside Estes Park. Getting away on weekends and pitching a tent in the park was truly wonderful. I even took up a small amount of rock climbing. One weekend I decided to head north from Fort Morgan and climb the Pawnee Buttes located in the Pawnee National Grasslands area. I successfully climbed one of the buttes and spent the night on top sleeping in a sleeping bag. It was a beautiful night on top of the butte sharing space with eagles and other high soaring birds. During my time on top of the butte, I had time to think about my life and decided I no longer wanted to work tall heights on commercial construction projects. The work was dangerous and I was constantly living out of cheap hotels or short-term kitchenette style rentals.

My desire was to head back to Illinois and find work somewhere in the local area of our home town. I desired to be around some past friends that were still in the area. I also wanted to find a job not as dangerous as my current construction job and not live on the road one hundred percent of the time. During the next two weeks on the job site I gave my notice to the job foreman about moving back home. A couple of the carpenters tried talking me out of the "idea" but to no avail. Within three weeks I was back in Illinois but this time with enough money in my pocket to afford an apartment and live my own life. After getting settled into an apartment, I looked up some past friends and started asking about work in the area. I quickly learned of a beef kill slaughterhouse located about twelve miles northwest of town. I was told they were hiring and I should put in an application. There was no stigma about slaughterhouses at the time and it sounded as good as any other job opportunity. I never imagined this slaughterhouse employment would change my life forever.

Thoughts for You

I was internally lost and doing what I had to do to survive. At the time I believed living on the open road and being homeless was worth the risk rather than living under my father's wrath. I do not condone this type of living, running away from problems, or disrespecting your parents. Moving from one labor intensive job to another across multiple states was not the best way to find and support myself. I was searching for the next best opportunity only to realize the opportunity was just another job that I really didn't want. Sure, these jobs put food on the table and provided basic shelter, but there were no goals or objectives beyond the basics. I was searching for something but didn't know what or how to get it. My prior home life gave me very little direction other than "Get a job, boy." There was never guidance at home or in high school about my potential. With a weak education it was difficult to envision myself providing greater value in society than what I already had been doing. Street smarts only got me so far and I needed better work. I wanted work that provided more stability with less risk. I wanted work that paid more than just getting by on a day to day basis. I also learned to be very careful who you befriend and who you spend your free time with.

Do you envision yourself in the same light? Does the job you are performing right now provide you a stepping stone to something better - either within the existing company or outside the company? Or do you believe there is nowhere else to go? Do your friends support your working and personal integrity ideals? Look around your work life and do your best to envision yourself with a better job that provides more money for yourself and greater support for you and/or your family. Within your circle of friends, ask yourself if any of them would support you unconditionally during periods of loss, suffering or great reward. Put a short-term plan into action and do your best to achieve that next career or personal position in life.

******

"Life is what we make it, always has been, always will be". Grandma Moses

Chapter 5 - Stories From the Slaughterhouse

Fresh Meat

Driving out to the slaughterhouse I was eager to put in a job application. Past experience working with and maintaining farm livestock, plus my experiences in the commercial construction industry made the transition to working in a slaughterhouse a normal progressive process. Though I was willing to work in this environment, a couple of my local friends told me to stay away from jobs directly related to the kill floor and rendering departments. Upon arrival at the plant I was directed to a small room where I filled out the respective job application. After a short waiting period I was then directed into the plant manager's office. A brief discussion about my farming and construction jobs led to a couple of inside phone calls to various department managers. The first department manager I met during the interview process was in charge of the Offal department. The definition of the word "offal" is "the organs (such as the liver or kidney) of an animal that are used for food" (http://www.merriam-webster.com/dictionary/offal). I had no idea what offal was, but it sounded a lot better than working the kill floor. The plant manager asked the offal department manager if he was short-handed or could use someone like myself. The manager sized me up and said, "Yes – let's have him start on Monday."

The slaughterhouse facility supported about two hundred twenty-five employees. This included employees in the cattle pens, kill floor, rendering, laundry, knife shop, loading docks, coolers, offal, fabrication and management offices. In 1974 the facility was considered one of the largest and most productive cattle based slaughterhouses in Illinois. The plant would process between one thousand two-hundred and one thousand four hundred-fifty head of cattle inside a nine hour day. There was great pride in attaining the higher numbers because this meant the processing line was continuously running with little or no stoppages from the United States Department of Agriculture (USDA) inspectors or by mechanical breakdowns. The plant's butcher workmen were unionized under the watchful eyes of the Amalgamated Meat Cutters and Butcher Workmen of North America – Post 787. This labor union represented the retail butchers and packinghouse laborers across North America.

Each union job was based upon seniority. Since I was the new guy, I was labeled as "fresh meat" with zero seniority. To move from one job to another required bidding on the open position. All bids were posted on the job board located along the hallway just outside the cafeteria. If you were interested in a particular job inside your department all you had to do was write your name on the open bid list. The person with the most seniority won. However, to transfer between departments your seniority in your existing department didn't transfer to the targeted department. This meant you must be willing to accept a lower paying and often terrible job that's available in the targeted department. There were very few inter-department bids.

Offal Jobs

Trimming Tongues

My Monday start date arrived and my starting time was 6:30 a.m. to allow for a quick introduction to the plant. I knew from my previous jobs that I was accountable so showing up at 6:30 a.m. was not a problem. I showed up appropriately and was fitted for "whites" which is what everyone called the white uniforms. I was also fitted for boots, gloves, white hard hat, knives with scabbard and sharpening steel, and a hair net. I was then walked out onto the kill floor where I was introduced to a worker who was working on the head and tongue line. I was really upset because I knew I didn't want to work the kill floor! What ever happened to working in the Offal department? I quickly learned this particular job was listed in the Offal department but located on the kill floor.

So, there I was standing in the middle of the kill floor, learning how to trim side meat off beef tongues but working in Offal. My job was to cut the designated side meat off the tongues and drop it in an adjoining two hundred gallon stainless steel barrel. The beef tongues were hanging next to their adjoining heads on a separate processing line from the rest of the steer. Each steer head and tongue was tagged with matching numbers to identify their place of origin. The line moved quickly which required my utmost attention to keeping my skinning knives constantly sharp and ensuring I didn't fall behind the line pace. If I fell behind then no product would be appropriately cut from the side of the beef tongue thereby creating a shortage of meat in the adjoining

61

stainless steel barrel. Too many shortages and you would receive a pink slip. After three pink slips you were suspended from work without pay. This was not a good situation for any rookie butcher workman. Since trimming tongues was my first job, I knew it would take months before I could bid myself out of the kill floor environment. This took resilience and accountability, and I was up to the challenge.

Slaughterhouse Rule - Accountability

In the slaughterhouse and working the kill floor line meant being on time every day and every hour. Employees had to punch the clock inside a fourteen minute window. This meant you can "punch in" from seven minutes prior to the top of the hour to seven minutes past the top of the hour. Our top of the hour time was 7 a.m. If you punched in too early you were counted as an unexcused absence. If you punched in too late then you were considered late. Being late three or more times within a thirty day period gives you a day off from work without pay.

Accountability was demanded at every job to ensure the daily working processes ran smooth and without error. The trimming tongues job was no exception. You were accountable for the knife in your hand and working machines so dangerous they could slice off a finger, hand or arm in the blink of an eye. As a butcher workman you were accountable to ensure your workspace was kept clean and in proper working order, lest a government inspector would tag your work area and cause the entire process to stop. Stopping the process meant temporarily shutting down production thereby losing the company money on a minute by minute basis. Time is money!

Slaughterhouse Rule – Integrity

Do what you say and say what you do – that's integrity. In the slaughterhouse you damn well better stand behind what you say to people because they will hold you to your word sooner or later. If you stated you were going to do something and didn't do it, you were viewed as not having integrity. In the business world you would be labeled as an "empty suit."

A large percentage of workers would bring their lunch to work. Too many times I heard about a co-workers lunch being stolen, which indicated a true lack of integrity in the guilty party. If you got caught stealing you would most likely pay the consequences either through suspension without pay or job loss on the spot. You would also be labeled by your co-workers as a thief, blacklisted and never trusted again. Gaining integrity as perceived by other employees took time. Consistently making mistakes or blaming others for poor work performance would guarantee a loss of integrity.

Pushing Meat

After eight months of trimming tongues out on the kill floor, a job opened up inside Offal and I bid on it. The job was called pushing meat. It's one of those jobs nobody wants. This job required excellent manipulation of a two-wheeled cart and moving two hundred gallon stainless steel barrels filled with offal product back into the Offal department. The job also included pushing and pulling large stainless steel rolling tubs and other related meat carrying devices filled with offal product. My job was to go out on the kill floor, collect the various barrels and other containers filled with offal product and bring them

63

back into the offal department for processing. I also had to help the scaler empty all the containers. The trick was keeping up with kill floor production while maintaining a constant flow of offal product to the receiving party (the person operating the weigh scale known as the scaler). Products picked up out on the kill floor were cheek meat, heart meat, oxlips, oxtails, head meat, spleens, and livers. When brought into Offal, I was also responsible to help the scaler empty out each barrel or tub. This job was very physically demanding and included walking miles in and around the kill floor and Offal departments every day. The kill floor was hot, humid and noisy while the Offal department was cold and dry. Plus many areas of the floor were slippery and demanded careful balance and control when moving product. After months of working my butt off pushing meat, I became very adept at working with the two-wheeled cart, manipulating heaving barrels of product and keeping up with the kill floor processes. The job had become mundane and I was looking for something else to do.

Slaughterhouse Rule - Resilience

I can absolutely guarantee you one thing about the slaughterhouse environment, you will work your butt off until the time comes that your specific function ("job") becomes automatic to your senses. There is no easy job in this space, only blood, sweat, and tears. Resilience in the slaughterhouse meant learning a new job, such as pushing meat, very quickly then becoming an "expert" at that particular job. This process took time with a strong level of resilience. As with any new job it's a major change in your work life. It takes time to master the new position. During this new phase of learning, you find yourself

64

working very hard to keep up with production line processes. However, once mastered, the job becomes thoughtless, mundane and physically easy.

The Floater

I had been at the plant for about one and one-half years working inside the Offal department. I was a good employee with a very consistent attendance record. I was accountable, showed respect towards other employees and gained their respect, maintained my own integrity and had a high level of resilience. I was also in good favor of the department manager. I had already built a strong work ethic and my body and brain adjusted quickly because of my previous hard back breaking work from the farm and construction jobs. These past labor skills came in extra handy at the slaughterhouse, especially inside the Offal department. Plus I was very handy with my hands and could integrate myself into various jobs with little or no training. The Offal department manager knew about my work ethic, witnessed my ability to learn quickly, and decided to move me around to different departmental jobs whenever someone called in sick or took some vacation time. I had gained his trust and respect. If I weren't pushing meat, I was filling in for someone who was not showing up for work. By default, I ended up being a floater across the many different jobs in Offal. This included managing and driving the department's loading dock forklift and transferring frozen products in and out of the freezer. I still had my regular job, but when someone missed a day I would be pulled from pushing meat and put in as the fill-in or floater. I enjoyed the variability and learning challenges between the Offal department jobs. However, from my perspective most of the jobs were boring and required minimal mental skill. Some jobs I liked more than others but there were three jobs I really didn't like. The three jobs I despised the most were scaling tripe, trimming lungs and breaking down tripe.

Scaling Tripe

The scaling tripe job was located in the hot, wet and smelly tripe room. Scaling tripe was the pits. Tripe is the stomach of the steer and quite large in size. You were required to lift the heavy wet tripe out of the floor bin and place it in the box on the scale. Each box was filled with tripe until it weighed anywhere from eighty to ninety pounds. The boxes were then stacked onto a wooden pallet with four boxes per row, five rows per pallet. Between each row a four foot by four foot corrugated plastic spacer was placed to ensure each row of boxes were air gapped for quick, even and effective freezing. If you didn't have a strong back or couldn't put up with wet, slimy and smelly water mixed with tripe juice all over your body then you were in for a very, very long day.

Trimming Lungs

The table for trimming lungs was located just behind the tripe scaling position inside the tripe room. The trick with this job was maintaining a very sharp skinning knife. The blood and fat mixed in between the lungs and the esophagus was nasty stuff. On top of that you had the tripe smell and heat mixed into the room. The job required cutting off all unnecessary fat and esophageal organs from the lungs and then placing each lung in a box until the box weighed approximately sixty pounds. The person operating the tripe scale was required to weigh each box of lungs and palletize them accordingly. On a daily basis the trimming lungs job was effectively managed by a large Greek man who consistently showed up to work on time, took little vacation and kept to himself. This was good news for me because I very seldom had to fill in for the "Greek". As already mentioned, the lung trimming job required maintaining a very sharp skinning knife otherwise this job quickly turned into a hot, sticky, smelly, wet and sweaty hell.

Breaking down Tripe

Those three words "breaking down tripe" made everyone in the Offal department run for cover. This was the most hated job in the department. After the tripe was boxed, weighed and palletized the product was placed in the freezer via forklift. You may recall each row of tripe had a plastic spacer to ensure quick and even freezing of all boxes on the pallet. When tripe was sold to third party companies it had to be completely frozen and "dead stacked" on new pallets. This meant that you had to re-stack the frozen tripe on a new pallet while removing the spacer between each row from the old pallet. The plastic spacers were then cleaned and re-used. This new stacked pallet of tripe was re-strapped (banded with nylon straps) onto its pallet and loaded into a refrigerated truck via forklift. Each pallet of tripe weighed approximately two thousand pounds and each semi-truck load of product was calculated at forty thousand pounds (twenty tons). The maximum limit for a forty foot trailer is forty thousand pounds. Therefore each semi-truck would haul twenty full pallets of frozen tripe. This might not sound all that bad. However, boxes of tripe are big, heavy and the tripe juice easily leaked out of the boxes. When pallets of tripe were stacked on top of each other in the freezer, due to the extreme weight, the box's tripe juice would leak down to the pallet below. The tripe juice would drip and run all over the pallet including all pallets stacked below. The juice would then freeze over and between the boxes. To successfully re-stack the tripe, many boxes had to be pried or beaten apart using meat hooks. Breaking down tripe was a cold, wet, smelly and back breaking job.

The Loading Dock

During my tenure as the meat pusher I had spent part of my time loading semi-truck trailers on the loading dock. Working the loading dock turned out to be one of my floating jobs. On a normal day the department manager would rustle up a few unsuspecting Offal employees and have them meet at the loading dock. Whatever product was to be shipped out that day had to be loaded onto the semi-truck trailers. All offal products loaded onto semi-truck trailers were dead stacked onto the trailer floor with the exception of tripe. As previously stated, tripe was re-stacked and banded onto individual pallets. Also, all offal products were processed through the freezer and frozen solid prior to shipment. There was not a defined job or job description for loading offal product trucks, most likely because the job was deemed as part-time. There were some days when multiple shipments of product were scheduled. Everyone in Offal already had full time daily jobs. If you wanted to earn a little overtime (time and a half past eight hours) you could volunteer to help load a truck down at the loading dock. After the normal work shift, many Offal employees would volunteer but worked as slow as possible thereby milking the clock for its overtime benefit. The kill floor was increasing its daily production and the loading dock got busier. As the number of trucks to load increased, it became more difficult to ship offal product on time without having to pay overtime to other employees.

One day I noticed a new Offal department job posted on the job board. It was for loading trucks on the loading dock. The job also entailed keeping track of manifests, ensuring weights and measures were correct plus overall cleaning and maintenance of the loading dock area. As the default departmental floater, I had the most experience loading trucks. I decided to bid on the job. Everyone thought I was crazy because loading trucks was cold, heavy, back breaking work. Spending days inside refrigerated truck trailers picking up and dead stacking boxes weighing between thirty to ninety pounds is not considered a good job. The pay was a bit higher than pushing meat, it removed me from the kill floor and our manager told me I got to monitor my own quality of work. Plus it was something different. After the required two-week posting period I won the job (I was the only employee to bid on the job) and started my new position on the loading dock.

My new position was highly physically demanding. I went home from work every day physically exhausted. It was one box at a time, one pallet at a time, one truck at a time. The days were long and hard with just me inside refrigerated trailers busting my butt. Every day I kept working the loading dock my body and mental position adjusted to the demands of the work. My resilience didn't waver and my accountability remained strong. I became a trusted friend with the fork lift driver, and he watched how I struggled to pick up hundreds of boxes each day and grew to respect my position. After three months on the dock my experience and physicality made truck loading look easy. I learned tricks and short cuts for picking up and moving heavy frozen boxes of product, thereby turning a nine hour day into a six or seven hour day. On average I would load two or maybe three trucks per day – depending upon the type of product. When trucks were not going out I would resume my old default job as the department floater. I had earned the respect of the department manager who gave me full responsibility for managing my working hours. Many of the Offal employees would see me taking long breaks or just hanging out in the break room. They became quite envious of my new found freedoms. What they didn't know was how hard I worked to earn the privileges.

The loading dock was getting busy with more products being sold, which meant more trucks needed loading. I had been loading trucks alone for about one year. The department manager decided to put up a second truck loader job posting. Fortunately for me, a young man fresh out of high school was recently hired into the department and decided to bid on the job. I now had a side-kick to train as a truck loader. As with me this young man went through the physically demanding learning pains of picking up heavy boxes of frozen product on a daily basis. Within two months of working together we could dead stack a full forty thousand pound load in forty minutes. Our manager was impressed with our work and wagered a bet. He bet us a case of beer we couldn't load an entire truck of cheek meat in thirty minutes or less. The bet was on and we began loading a forty thousand pound truck load of check meat at eighty pounds per box. The final time was thirty minutes and thirty eight seconds. We lost the bet, but our manager shared the case of beer.

186,000 Pounds

During the middle of a work week, our manager was beginning to talk about a very busy Friday on the loading dock. The busiest loading day of the work week seemed to fall on Friday's. Our starting time was always 7 a.m. Upon arrival I learned indeed there were many loads to go out for the Friday work day. The manifests were printed out and our loading strategy for the day came alive. In the list there were three full loads of tripe – the most difficult loads for us to work. We decided to first break down tripe for all three loads and prepare the first three trucks specifically for tripe loads. On that Friday the two of us loaded a total of nine semi-truck trailers of offal product. This was accomplished inside nine hours, a new loading record for the Offal department's loading dock. At forty to forty-five thousand pounds per truck (some trucks were forty five feet in length and could accept more weight) and nine trucks that meant we picked up and dead stacked three hundred sixty- thousand pounds of frozen products. Add another twelve thousand pounds for the extra-long trucks, pallets and miscellaneous docking gear and the total was three hundred seventy-two thousand pounds inside nine hours. The total weight I picked up in one nine hour day was one hundred eighty-six thousand pounds! I have never picked up that much weight in a single

71

day's work since. My loading dock mate and I went out for a couple of beers that night. We were tired but not broken.

The Freezer

The freezer was the opposite environment of a hot hell. It was a large rectangular box with a solid concrete floor, six overhead refrigeration units, and capable of holding up to one million pounds of product. The freezer was designed to maintain a temperature of minus thirty-two degrees Fahrenheit below zero. Poorly designed, the freezer's refrigeration units would defrost on a regularly scheduled basis. Each unit's water draining system would freeze up after the first defrost cycle so all the water would run down onto the palletized products sitting below, and then onto the floor. This created uneven ice sheets across the floor and froze multiple pallets of products together. Plus, the tripe bay was constantly leaking tripe juice and freezing onto the floor too. The unevenness of the floor created great difficulty with transferring pallets of product around with the forklift. Any load going in or out of the freezer was constantly shifting on the forklift forks. It took many weeks of diligent practice to become a skilled forklift driver in the freezer.

After the freezer was closed up each weekend and by Monday morning the temperature would be around minus thirty eight degrees Fahrenheit below zero. Opening the freezer door on Monday mornings was always an interesting experience. The freezer would look like a frozen rectangular ice cave, something right out of a Hollywood movie. Driving the forklift into the freezer first thing Monday morning would take your breath away. To access the freezer on Monday mornings, sometimes I had to chop ice away from the door using a ten pound steel bar that had one end sharpened. Manipulating pallets of product required getting off the forklift and chopping ice off the floor and/or around the pallets of products. The longest single time period I spent in the freezer without coming out was one hour and twenty minutes. When I finally came out I looked like the frozen walking dead.

It was a brutal and harsh environment with only the most skilled forklift drivers allowed to manage the frozen product. I became one of the skilled forklift drivers. I believed if I could drive a forklift in this environment on highly uneven slippery surfaces and keep up with production I could drive a forklift anywhere. Many times boxes of product would fall from a pallet while the pallet of product was fifteen feet to twenty feet up in the air. An incident happened when the forklift was listing heavily to the left and multiple eighty pound boxes of frozen tripe fell onto the forklift. One of the boxes landed directly onto my right calf muscle tearing it apart. I spent the next month on crutches, in physical therapy and missing work. At minus thirty two degrees Fahrenheit below zero with highly uneven surfaces this particular freezer was a dangerous proposition for any forklift driver.

Full Circle

There were many other offal jobs I performed. For example, Offal had an edible rendering department that collected and melted the animal fat, ran it through a centrifuge then pumped it into large stainless steel vats. From these large vats the pure liquid fat would be transferred into an awaiting tanker truck. The animal fat was used to manufacture

73

cooking oils, makeup, or anything needing an animal oil base acceptable for human consumption. I learned how to manage this job too.

I would be remiss in your education about the slaughterhouse if I didn't discuss other components about the working production of the slaughterhouse itself. For example, the steer would walk in on all four hoofs and within twenty six minutes become two half sides of beef hanging in a thirty four degree cooler. Every piece of product extracted from the animal via the kill floor was sold on the open market. This included anything that was swept or hosed off the floor. The processing of the animal was highly efficient leaving nothing behind. Everyone's job within the production cycle was just as important as the job to the person's right or left. To most people in the outside world, the slaughterhouse was a very gruesome place to work.

USDA government inspectors constantly focused on finding unwanted bacteria or problems with a specific lot of cattle. All cattle were sequentially tagged to enable tracking of the product from your kitchen table back to its origin: the farmer. Each inspector was educated to accurately notice any subtle changes in product color to help detect an abnormality that would make the product unsafe for human consumption. I held the inspectors in high regard and always performed my job to meet or exceed their requirements.

Between the kill floor and fabrication departments were large coolers where half sides of beef would hang covered with nylon shrouds. From the coolers the half sides would be rolled on overhead rails to the fabrication department. This department turned the sides of beef into steaks, hamburger or whatever was being sold on the market. Some of

74

the half sides would be cut into quarters and hinds for selling direct to large grocery store butcher shops or distribution centers. All products were loaded and hauled onto refrigerated trucks that maintained a specified temperature. This is where your red steer meat was fabricated, sold, and transported.

It Takes All Types

Work life in the slaughterhouse encompassed many different types of people from all aspects of society. About two thirds of the workers were Caucasian with the rest split between Hispanic and African American. Most jobs did not require much formal education. The majority of unionized employees had high school diplomas but no other formalized education. There were a number of illegal immigrants working inside the plant too. My logical guess is between five to ten percent of employees were illegal immigrants. The illegals were hard working, kept to themselves and always showed up for work. During my tenure the state police and Immigration & Naturalization Service (INS) showed up at the plant on two separate occasions. If you were illegal you were seen running for the doors. To my surprise the majority of the illegal immigrants caught and deported showed up for work again within three months.

Violence

There were those individuals who didn't work well with others. These people seemed to have a chip on their shoulders about everything in life. Unfortunately for many good and hard-working employees, these bad apples created havoc inside various departments. If a fight broke out on the kill or fabrication floors it usually ended in a fist fight. Most fights were quickly squelched by floor foreman and their management team. However, there were occasions when knives were drawn. These altercations ended in either one person relenting, running away or getting stabbed. I remember when a very large (about six foot four-inches, two hundred-fifty pounds) and highly uneducated man was constantly being harassed by another employee of smaller stature. They both worked in the fabrication department. During a morning break and inside the main hallway just outside the cafeteria this mountain of a man went berserk, picked up the guy harassing him, and slammed his upper body into a glass gravity box mounted on the hallway wall. He then proceeded to hit and beat anyone near him. I was on my break and standing no more than thirty feet away. I was standing next to my loading dock mate when the Offal manager yelled "Let's get him." It took four of us men to wrestle this guy to the floor and hold him down until he agreed to leave the plant without further altercation. About two hours later this man re-appeared at the plant with a shotgun and looking for revenge. Luckily for us, the guards were well prepared, the state police showed up within minutes and the man was arrested without incident.

Slaughterhouse Rule - Respect

Slaughterhouse respect is somewhat different. This is because the application and quality of your job is consistently being watched by floor foremen, assistant foremen and United States Department of Agriculture (USDA) inspectors. You must show and give respect to the foremen and their USDA counterparts while on the job, every hour of every day. As the department's floater and owing to the quality of my work, I had gained respect from other employees, management and the inspectors. Respect also came from respecting those butcher workmen who had been working the slaughterhouse for decades. These were the seasoned veterans. Most (but not all) of the seasoned veterans would help train and cross-train the new employees. Those seasoned veterans who helped were looked upon with great respect. There was zero tolerance for disrespect.

Slaughterhouse Rule - Trust

Be the best you can be at your job. The rule of trust in the slaughterhouse meant you performed your job to the best of your abilities at all times. I worked very hard as the departmental floater to ensure the quality of work I produced was accepted by the inspectors and management. I consistently produced top quality work and gained the trust of management, because when I filled in for another employee the job was done right. You didn't slack off or continuously make known mistakes. In the slaughterhouse you are part of a systemic process. If you performed shoddy work someone downstream in the process pays for it. Therefore, each individual "trusted" that every other individual performed their job/task to the utmost of their ability with the best quality. No slackers here! The consequences were significant amongst your peers.

Thoughts for You

For me, work life in the slaughterhouse was quite eventful. There was always more work to be accomplished in a single day than could be done. Moving around from job to job as the temporary fill-in person reduced the amount of mundane work and monotony experienced with working on a manufacturing line. The variability in jobs worked well for me.

As a process oriented manufacturing facility, all jobs depended upon sustained factory processes. If any process failed within the chain of manufacturing this affected all other jobs. Therefore, it was critical to ensure each employee could perform their function at a high quality level. Fortunately for me I had the innate ability to perform any job inside the Offal department at a quality level acceptable by management.

My past learning experiences on the farm, working closely with farm animals, and the difficult work on commercial construction sites fitted well within the slaughterhouse culture. Once I became accustomed to the environment my skill sets blossomed. I didn't know I could perform all the jobs until I dedicated and focused my physical skills to the job presented to me. The line jobs required physical stamina to perform the same repetitive task(s) for eight plus hour a day which was a non-issue for me.

Do you find yourself saying "I could do that" or "I should be doing that job?" Are you leveraging your innate skill sets to get ahead in your current work environment, whether it's white or blue collar? Do you believe you can perform the job but have not been given the opportunity to prove yourself? If you have the internal desire and willingness to take the step forward, I believe your work life value can blossom. Targeting that next position takes an action plan and requires focused execution with the willingness and determination to achieve your objectives. It's great to have work goals, but meeting your own objectives will become the stepping stones to achieving those goals. Create an action plan and start working towards that next bigger and better opportunity. You can do it!

*****

"If you do what you've always done, you'll get what you've always gotten." Tony Robbins

Chapter 6 - Life's Forces and the Big Plan

Local People

Biker Buddies

Working at the slaughterhouse was paying dividends for me as a single man living in a small apartment. I had low monthly expenses which enabled me to save money for emergencies or purchasing a recreational vehicle such as a motorcycle. It was now the summer of 1975 and I was forming closer relationships with past acquaintances. Linking up with two of my past farm buddies I found out they were into Harley Davidson motorcycles. I fell in love with the thought of riding my own Harley with friends and acting out our freedoms to the limit. I saved back some money and by December could afford a down payment. I purchased an XLH 1000 Harley Davidson Sportster motorcycle from a local automobile dealer who showed it in their front window. Apparently, the previous owner was backing the motorcycle out of his garage, lost his balance, and when the Harley toppled over it broke one of his legs. He immediately traded in the Harley for a pickup truck. The Harley had only five hundred miles on it and was in new condition being sold at a discounted price. Although I was dying to tear up some pavement, I stored the bike until early Spring when the weather warmed up. I also had enough money to upgrade my older pickup truck to a newer model.

A couple of my ex-farm buddies were living the life of "snow birds." They lived in Phoenix, Arizona during the winter months and lived in the hometown throughout spring, summer, and fall. When in town we would get together and ride our Harleys all over northwest Illinois. Between these two farm hand friends and a couple other guys from the slaughterhouse who owned Harleys, we created our own biker group. Here we were a small group of young men with long hair riding Harleys and rolling through small towns of northern Illinois. On multiple occasions when stopping for fuel or getting a bite to eat, either a local cop or highway patrolman would pull up and ask for the usual paperwork. They also liked following us until we were far enough outside of town until we appeared not to be a threat. We all got a laugh out of these situations as we were just ex-farm boys enjoying our new found freedom, which consisted of clearing my thoughts of working in the slaughterhouse while enjoying the wind in my face along less traveled country highways.

A Local Gal

On a warm Friday night I was playing some pool and having a beer at the local bar. I noticed a fine single woman standing in the corner and approached her with interest. She was a local person just like me. We started dating on a regular basis and found ourselves spending a lot of free time together. We enjoyed the current music scene (disco), traveling to rock and roll concerts, riding my Harley, and staying out drinking and dancing into the late hours. With little to do in a very small town it was just a matter of time before alcohol, heated passion and being human got the best of us. About six months after my twentieth birthday my girlfriend was pregnant with our baby. We were excited and held great anticipation about having a baby. Three weeks before my twenty first birthday we got married. Then three months later our daughter was born. These events, all significant, seemed to happen very quickly. I immediately bonded with our baby girl and she became the "Apple of my eye." I was very happy and over the top elated to be a father to a beautiful baby girl.

There I was working full time at the slaughterhouse, married with a family and I just turned twenty-one! I was also the primary wage earner, which put us just above the poverty line. Being young and immature did not help our relationship. Our marriage was never made in heaven. Unfortunately, it was filled with animosity, yelling, screaming and poor communication skills between two very young adults. How did my parents do it? Behind closed doors a home is not always happy. From my perspective we were not suited as marriage partners but we both felt strongly that marriage was the right thing to do when raising our child.

Looking for Normalcy

Both of us managed to maintain a perceived level of normalcy outside of our home and work. We took our daughter everywhere and rarely hired a baby sitter. We would visit grandparents and cousins from both sides of the family, attend family reunions and actively attend social and church sponsored events. As a family we began supporting the local Jaycee chapter, the United States Junior Chamber of Commerce. This organization supports leadership training with emphasis on management skills, business development and community services.

Through the Jaycees we did a ton of volunteering and helping those individuals less fortunate than ourselves. The local Jaycee chapter was a good outlet for me as a young man with an unknown future. As a volunteer one of our projects was clearing dead hardwood trees from local farmers' land. The trees would be cut up with our chain saws then each log split with a log splitter. We would build large piles of hardwood fire wood in preparation of the upcoming winter months. During the winter months we would sell the wood for seventy-five dollars a pickup truck load which included hauling and stacking the fire wood on the customer's property.

I especially enjoyed our Halloween haunted house event and volunteered as the haunted house project chairman. This was a daunting task because the chapter had been losing money sponsoring a haunted house for the previous three years. Due to the financial losses, the chapters' Board of Directors was talking about scraping the annual project. When I became the chair person, all eyes were on me to deliver a haunted house project that made money for the community. During the next three years as the haunted house chairman our chapter earned many thousands of dollars. From this success, I decided to run for a local office position. I became the local Jaycee chapter State Director. This meant traveling to other Jaycee chapters and promoting volunteerism across our many programs. As an active Jaycee member I was learning the fundamentals about how to manage projects, give presentations and collaborate with local community leaders.

Between working full time at the slaughterhouse, raising and supporting a family and being actively involved in the local Jaycee chapter, I was a very busy young man. There was not much time spent thinking about the future or planning anything beyond the existing reality of my life's forces. I didn't earn enough money to invest in a financial future that would sustain our family above and beyond our existing lifestyle. Work seemed to be nothing more than what it was – mundane, hard, sweaty and back breaking never ending work. On a daily basis I would interact with men in their early fifties who have been working the slaughterhouse business their entire working lives. Their bodies were already breaking down and they looked much older than their years. Was this going to be me in thirty years?

The relationship with my wife was mentally taxing. We would argue about everything. Given our young ages we were both too stubborn and ignorant to know how to compromise and fight a good fight. We didn't realize that it's normal to disagree about various elements in your relationship, but to do it respectfully. We both worked hard to maintain a good and stable environment for our daughter. It takes more than just hard work to keep a marriage afloat. It takes the slaughterhouse rules plus empathy, caring of one another, and a passion for love. For us, the slaughterhouse rules cycled in and out of our relationship but empathy, love and a caring mindset was minimal at best. My life had become a level of emotional misery above and beyond what I could manage.

Reality Bites

At the age of twenty-three, despite the delights of a two year old to make me smile each day, I began to wonder where my life was going.

I envisioned my work holding no future, living within an unwanted marriage, and having no clue what to do with my life. I witnessed my ex-farm buddies moving on in their lives by obtaining sustainable work with the Illinois Department of Transportation. They managed to purchase some farm land with homes in the local area and create a very nice sustainable and secure life for themselves and their families. I experienced a few of my past high school acquaintances moving back into the local community after graduating college. They were either starting up small businesses or obtaining management jobs with companies in the region. Seeing their successes I began asking the question "What am I doing with my life?" I felt almost embarrassed at how I was earning a living. I wanted to improve myself so I could better support my family, but had no idea how to do it.

In addition to my future-less job and living in an unwanted marriage, the local region was experiencing a significant financial downturn. The regional job market had plummeted due to the cut-backs at the local farm implement factories such as John Deere, Case, and International Harvester. There was a gas shortage with waiting lines to get your automobile filled up. Interest rates on home mortgages were hovering at thirteen percent and rising. With these financial pressures, I found myself attending multiple funerals of young men who lived and worked in the community. These young men were victims of drug overdoses, drunken driving accidents, suicide (seven in two years) and just plain ignorance. The reality of my personal and work life was slowly closing in on me and putting negative pressure on my outlook to the future.

A Divorce

The relationship with my wife continued to deteriorate. Our arguing had become mentally and physically abusive. I believed that sooner or later one of us would pull the plug and we'd go our separate ways. After two plus years of living in a very painful relationship I decided it was time to separate. After a normal workday, I came home and bravely told my wife that I was moving out in two weeks and would be seeking a divorce. She looked at me in disbelief, laughed in my face and walked away. She did not broach the subject again until the weekend came when I started packing my clothes. Again in disbelief she started laughing and screaming at me. She kept telling me how much of a loser I was and I would never see my daughter again. Deep inside I knew she would leverage our daughter against me but I kept packing and immediately moved to an awaiting one bedroom apartment. I contacted a local lawyer to obtain legal advice and found out we would have to be separated for one full year and then I was eligible for a divorce filing. During this one year time period I maintained a self-appointed child support program and did my best to negotiate visitation time with our daughter. My soon to be ex-wife was bitter, resentful, and as anticipated, used our daughter against me. I managed to spend a few hard fought negotiated hours a week with our daughter. The stress my wife put upon me was so severe it was almost palpable. For stress relief I fell back on my cross country running days in high school. Like a Forest Gump character I would hit the open road and run to almost exhaustion. The distance running helped me clear my mind of negative thoughts and

86

relieve the work and personal stresses in my life. I found myself running thirty to fifty miles a week and having more running shoes than any other shoes in my closet. One year later to the day of filing separation papers, I filed for divorce.

Positive Influences

A Government Inspector

For many successful people there is a person (mentor), a serendipitous incident, or a combination of the two that had a positive and profound effect on their lives. Fortunately, they both came into my life at the right time but in a very unusual environment: a tripe room inside a slaughterhouse.

I was working with another butcher workman in the tripe room when one of the USDA government inspectors stopped by and began talking to my workmate. Apparently their families knew each other from local social circles. I became interested in the conversation and stood alongside to listen. The inspector invited my workmate to stop by for an early dinner after work. I asked "Hey, what about me?" The inspector openly invited and added me to the dinner plans, then gave me directions to her home. What I didn't know was that this inspector and her family were well known in the area, highly respected, and lived in a beautiful home with adjoining property just outside of town. That dinner invitation and subsequent dinner invitations turned out to have a very profound and positive effect on my life.

Within a short period of time I began to share insights with my new inspector friend about my miserable marriage, how I wanted more out of life than working the slaughterhouse, and the lost feeling I had about my future. These discussions revealed my deep desire to move above and beyond my existing life and that deep inside me there was a better person waiting to be found. The problem was I had no idea how I was going to get out of my current life cycle, what I was going to do, where I was going, or how I was going to get there.

Over the next year I became good friends with this inspector, her family and a few of their friends. These new people in my life had a different mindset, and outlook about what life had to offer. The inspector became a mentor to me and encouraged me to think and reach beyond my current expectations. She was impressed with my quick wit and my willingness to tackle and effectively solve problems. She witnessed my ability to perform all the functions in the Offal department at the required quality level of the USDA. More than once she mentioned I should be in college and learning about management or engineering. With her positive influence I began thinking about how life would be working as an engineer. Within her family, I formed relationships of mutual trust and open communications. The inspector and her family (all family members had college degrees) were starting to have a strong positive impact on my life.

I started to envision college in my future. At their suggestion, I read a couple of books which I would like to share with you here today:

- Success Through a Positive Mental Attitude; by Napoleon Hill and W. Clement Stone

- Think and Grow Rich; by Napoleon Hill

I read these books with fervor and gained insight into a more positive attitude and outlook on life. I have these books in my book case today and use them as references.

A Navy Man

One day I was again invited over for an early after work dinner. To my delight my inspector friend's brother was visiting from California. Unlike anyone I had met before, he was an active duty Navy Captain stationed at Alameda Naval Air Station. I began asking a lot of questions, and over a beer or two I learned about the US Navy including some basics of its operational capabilities. For the first time in my life, I felt an interest in the military life – especially the Navy.

After his visit my new found Navy Captain friend telephoned me a couple of times. During one of the phone calls I began thinking about putting a plan in place that would help move my life into a more positive and forward direction – perhaps a Navy life? He also mailed me a packet of information about the Navy. The information packet listed many jobs available with submarines, surface ships, logistics, operations and intelligence. I quickly realized all top rated enlisted jobs in the Navy required a six year commitment. That was a curve ball I had not expected. Thinking about my future, I calculated I would need to commit to a six year Navy term plus another four years of college post my Navy enlistment. This ten year commitment didn't feel unsurmountable but was definitely viewed as a long stretch of time in my life cycle. I also quickly realized my educational level was well below the expected standards of establishing a decent rate (job) in the Navy. At the time it was a good idea but the reality of making such a far reaching change seemed outside of my existing reality.

The Big Plan

A key component of "The Big Plan" consisted of acquiring a college education in a field of study that I believed would sustain me for the rest of my working life. I had a strong internal desire to learn something new every day. I wanted to advance my knowledge and believed a college degree was my ticket to a better future and work life. For many different reasons, the greater majority of people in the United States and around the world don't go to college. For those individuals who work in factories, on farms, or have built their own business without an advanced formal education, my personal gratitude and respect goes out to you. Not everyone needs or wants to go to college to self-identify as being successful. Societies across the world have a strong need for people to work with their hands to build and make "stuff." If you are an individual who is an integral part of the blue collar workforce, please keep building, making and doing – we need you! I truly believed that a college education was my best personal exit from poverty level living and thinking. This is the path that I had desired, but it's not for everyone.

During the course of this very impactful year I kept discussing with my inspector friend about the limited options of my current life, and visualizing a very different future. Finally, I decided enough was enough and told my inspector friend that I wanted to go to college and

become an engineer. From my earlier conversations with her brother, I knew it would take me ten years to accomplish. This included serving my country for six of those years. I calculated I would then be thirty five years old. I accepted the fact that I could be thirty five with or without a college degree. It was my choice to make. I believed that earning an honorable discharge, then graduating from college with an engineering degree would open doors to other opportunities. I also believed this commitment would allow me to strive for a better life for my daughter and my own future. In my mind the sequence of events to accomplish this ten year plan was:

1. Qualify, then join the Navy
2. Quit my job
3. Earn an honorable discharge, then attend college
4. Graduate with an engineering degree

Depending upon the individual, each of these events could be considered major life changes. I knew the risk was high and the future unknown. I also knew if I didn't start making the changes now the chances of success diminished over time. I committed internally to make The Big Plan happen.

Join the Navy

The decision to join the Navy was a very difficult decision for me. I couldn't see myself living in the current small town with the same negative influences that had encircled my life. I believed that for me to be successful I had to leave the area and start a new life somewhere else. I envisioned the Navy was my ticket to start that new life.

Four months after my divorce was finalized, I met with a Navy recruiter. The Navy had a delayed entry program where the candidate could sign up but not report to boot camp until a future date. This delayed program was appealing to me. It would give me time to get my personal and financial affairs in order before reporting to boot camp. While meeting with the recruiter I told him I wanted to give my heart and soul to my country, learn electronics and save money for college. The recruiter was delighted with my response but was not interested with signing me unless I could pass their entrance exams. The exams included being tested on math, basic electronics and other lower level college criteria. With a low quality high school education my options were limited to remedial physical jobs. I was very disappointed, thinking there was no way I would get in the Navy at the level of opportunity I had desired.

I reached out to my inspector friend and she guided me in the direction to our local library. I knew absolutely nothing about how to find anything in a library or how to leverage a library as a learning tool. The last time I was in a library was during High School and I was kicked out due to fighting. Upon entering the local library a very nice librarian asked me if I needed help and what I was looking for. I said I needed to study up on math and electronics. She spent the next twenty minutes showing me where the math and electronics books were located. During my first visit I immediately signed up for my first library card. Over the next two months I visited the library at least a dozen times. I checked out the respective books and privately studied basic math and electronics. Much to my surprise I actually enjoyed learning about math, was good at understanding numbers and picked up on the properties and applicability of electronics very quickly.

After about two months of preparation I felt confident that I could pass the Navy's advanced entrance exams. I set a new appointment with the Navy recruiter to take the entrance exams. My final scores were high enough to qualify me for the Navy's Advanced Electronics Field (AEF) and if desired to take more exams to qualify for nuclear reactor training school. I learned that nuclear propulsion systems were only placed on aircraft carriers and submarines. I didn't want anything to do with either of those military platforms and nixed the idea of testing into the nuclear program. However, the AEF program was a definite "yes" and I immediately signed up for six years of active duty service. My service acceptance date was set at the future date of September 24, 1980. I had three months to get my personal and financial affairs in order. I was now set on course for a six year Navy term then four years of college. My ten year plan had just begun!

Quit My Job

Still working at the slaughterhouse like nothing had changed, and not telling anyone I had joined the Navy, was an enlightening experience. Every day I went to work I knew there would come a time when I would put my two week notice in and tell all of my workmates of my life's plan. Knowing there was a light at the end of the tunnel instilled a positive mental attitude within my mind. Likewise, my distance running had become automatic and had a definitive positive effect with my mental outlook too. My attitude about working became more positive and I was willing to perform any crappy job that crossed my path. I even went to the local barber and got a real hair cut! My hair was cut from shoulder length up to about the middle of my ears – a very definitive change. My working colleagues at the slaughterhouse looked at me like I was losing my mind or wondered what was going on in my life. I was in great shape mentally, physically and prepared for a major life change.

Finally the day came. I called out to four Offal department workers to gather around. I told them about my ten year plan, that I had joined the Navy, and put my two week notice into management. With looks of complete disbelief I was rewarded with laughs and told I was crazy. Once the news spread throughout the department, I was approached by many people with varying responses to the news. Some wished me luck while others looked down on me for quitting my job and being a narcissist. There were no parties given on my behalf, nor was there a feeling of support from my workmates and so-called friends. I guess the quote "Birds of a feather flock together" holds true in this instance and I was no longer of that feather. I had broken out from the pack. I quickly learned that I had three true friends who unconditionally supported me. None of these three individuals worked at the slaughterhouse.

I called my parents and said I wanted to stop by and share some news with them. When I walked into their home they were both sitting in the living room watching television. Standing in front of them I said I gave my two week notice at the plant and had joined the Navy. This was out of the blue information for them and coming from someone they

least expected. My father was quite surprised to hear the Navy accepted me until I told him about my part-time studies at the library and passing the entrance exams. Both of my parents excitedly absorbed the news and were delighted that I was putting myself forward, taking a risk and had an action plan to better my life. They knew about my difficulties with my now ex-wife and were concerned about my daughter – their only granddaughter. They asked me how I was going to support and maintain a relationship with my daughter. I told them about my existing financial support plan, but emotionally I would need help. They promised me they would watch carefully over my daughter and would support her mother the best they could during my absence.

Thoughts for You

We all have our local environments where we build and nurture personal and professional relationships. Within our local space we spend our time, our money and energy building our lives around and with others. You could be living in a first, second, or third tier city or in a small town/village. There can be negative and positive influences within any environment. From my small town bubble I was negatively influenced by short term thinkers, drugs, drinking, absence of outside knowledge and a poor grounding of spiritual guidance or beliefs. Positive influences in my life came from volunteerism, forming close bonds of friendship with successful people and reading books that guided me towards a different way of thinking. The point is there are positive and negative influences in your life right now that are capable of pulling you in multiple directions.

I was not actively seeking out individuals that would have a positive impact on my life. I did not know having an early dinner between friends would be a single event in my life that started a chain reaction of other life altering events. Looking back at those moments in time, I was fortunate to be in the right place at the right time with the right people. I did know that I was willing to accept the risk of making change in my life. I also knew I was accountable for my thoughts, actions, and ultimately how I affected my family and other people around me. Knowing I had to leave my daughter was excruciatingly painful. However, I believed in the long run the life changes would be better for my daughter and me and hoped to have the opportunity to rebuild a close relationship with her in the future.

When you plan and implement significant life changes, you find out who your friends truly are. You can usually count them on one hand. Think about the positive and negative influences placed upon you today. Make a list consisting of two columns showing positive influences on one side and negative influences on the other side. Ask yourself what actions you can take today that will consistently keep you moving towards the positive column. Maybe you will find a mentor or someone who will listen to your dreams unconditionally; or maybe you will find an organization that can help guide you toward a more rewarding life path. As Yogi Berra said "When you come to a fork in the road, take it." I believe this means that when presented a life altering decision, you should weigh both the positive and negative attributes, make your decision and, most importantly, move forward with commitment. When

I came to my fork in the road, I picked it up, put it in my pocket and headed towards a new life as a Navy man with a ten year plan.

*****

"Two roads diverged in a wood, and I – I took the one less traveled by, and that has made all the difference." Robert Frost

Chapter 7 - Military – All In

Boot Camp Stories

One month before my twenty-fifth birthday, I reported to Navy boot camp in Orlando, Florida. This particular boot camp supported both male and female enlisted Navy personnel. My first military experience began within ten minutes from exiting the bus. A sharply dressed young man wearing Navy boot camp working blues came outside and began barking orders to get in line, stand to attention, shut up and don't move. I quickly learned I had walked through a door not knowing what was on the other side. In a single moment I realized I was no longer classified as a civilian but as a low life, scum of the earth boot camp recruit. It felt like I was entering into an unknown country and having to learn a new culture and language.

Recruit Indoctrination Facility

For the next three days I lived in a dormitory type environment called the Recruit Indoctrination Facility (RIF). There were at least one-hundred young men sequestered into a large room. Inside the room were neatly arranged steel bunk bed style beds – our new sleeping quarters. These young men came from all walks of life and from every corner of the United States. Encircling the outer perimeter of the beds was a red line painted on the tile floor. Every morning between 03:30 hours and 04:30 hours (oh three-hundred thirty and oh four-hundred thirty military time) we were abruptly awakened by senior ranking boot camp recruits. They would begin each day by banging on steel garbage cans with broom handles, switch the lights off and on in rapid succession and play loud music from a portable music player blasting out the selected song of the morning. Unfortunately, some of the newly formed civilian recruits decided to party hard the last couple of nights before showing up for boot camp. They were not in good physical or mental shape to begin their boot camp training. The first morning while standing at attention on the red line could have been a scene from a Hollywood movie. There were men extremely hung over, throwing up on themselves while others were passing out and collapsing onto the hard tile floor. I could hear loud thuds when their bodies hit the floor. Medical staff was standing by and attending to the less fortunate while the rest of us were "volunteered" to clean up their messes. There was no drinking or partying for me on the eve of starting my Navy career. Instead, my last night before boot camp consisted of little sleep due to anxiety from fear, uncertainty and doubt. After two days of fun in RIF, I was ready, willing and waiting to be assigned to my new company.

During the mid-afternoon on the third day a company commander showed up and started calling names. Our boot camp recruit company was finally being formed. The company consisted of eighty-three recruits. My next stop was to get a haircut and acquire the required recruit working blue uniforms with accompanying boondockers (Navy boots). It was hot and humid in Orlando, during late September. Because of the heat and humidity, I was looking forward to getting my hair cut. We became men wearing the same uniforms with the same haircuts. Everyone was the same regardless of race, color, religion or political affiliation. The only identifying individualism was created by stenciling our last name and company number onto our uniforms. After getting our haircuts and a sea bag full of clothes, we marched over to our new barracks which were located on the third (top) floor of a multi-story building. Again, our living arrangement was a dormitory style environment with bunk beds consisting of one upper bed and one lower.

A Formalized Company of Recruits

The official first day in the company consisted of determining who was going to be assigned recruit leadership roles. These leadership roles consisted of Recruit Training Petty Officer, Master at Arms, Starboard Watch Petty Officer, Port Watch Petty Officer and the Recruit Chief Petty Officer (RCPO). Each recruit petty officer had an assigned job and was accountable for the various training, cleanliness and safety of all recruits in the company. The selection process was managed by the Company Commander and the Assistant Company Commander. A form was given to every recruit in the company. I filled out the form describing where I came from, last employment positions and the responsibilities of those positions. I wrote down that I worked in a slaughterhouse as a butcher workman and was the assistant to the department foreman. Within an hour my name was called and I had to report to the small attached office located at the end of the barracks – the Company Commander's office. While in the office the Company Commander asked me why I waited so long to join. I was almost twenty-five years old and the average age to join was between eighteen to twenty years of age. I explained that I wanted to support and defend my country while learning electronics and traveling the world. To my shock and surprise, I was immediately assigned as the Recruit Port Watch Petty Officer, otherwise known as the Port Watch. This was my first new military leadership position that I happily accepted!

My first responsibility as the Port Watch was to teach all the recruits on the port side of the barracks (half of the company) how to march. That was interesting as I had never marched a step in my life! I began studying a large three ring binder of marching instructions with accompanying boot camp protocols. Every night I would join the other company recruit petty officers in the Company Commander's office. Together, we learned about each other's new military duties while reminiscing about our past civilian lives. I formed a very solid bond with the RCPO and the Master at Arms. I would study and practice the marching protocols and steps, and began memorizing many aspects of the Uniform Code of Military Justice (UCMJ). There were specific codes we had to know by rote and be able to state them on a moment's notice anywhere at any time in any order. During the first week in the barracks we practiced folding our clothes, shining our boondockers and ensuring everything (I mean everything) was spit shining clean. This included cleaning the floor (deck), ceiling (overhead), walls (bulkheads), bathroom (head), bunking materials, clothing, and our bodies.

The Grinder

The grinder was a very large (maybe quarter mile by half mile wide) asphalt area where all companies of recruits learned how to march and take physical punishment from the Company Commanders and their assistants. I quickly learned that if it rained in the overnight, the grinder became the perfect place for wasting a clean set of dungarees and spit shined boots. Wherever there was dirty standing water that is where I found myself doing push-ups, sit ups and body builders. Between the dirty water, occasional mud hole and lots of sweat, my uniform was in constant disrepair and caked with mud. Every night we cleaned our bodies, uniforms and boots ensuring that our uniforms were dry and folded as per orders. Every day we would hit the grinder and the process would start all over again. As an ex-farm boy and slaughterhouse worker, the dirty water, mud and sweat did not bother me as it did with many other recruits. Because of my experience with distance running the long days marching didn't bother me either.

Carrying the Flag

Between marches we would run a mile (or for however long the Company Commander stated). During our runs we were required to keep in step with whoever was holding the company flag. One day the Company Commander told me to take the flag and start running. It was my turn to show the company what running was all about! I immediately started running at a six minute per mile pace and left about ninety percent of the company recruits behind. When the run was completed a small group of recruits pulled the flag out of my hands and told me to never touch it again! They were not happy with my performance and I obliged with their request. There were recruits that had a very difficult time running one mile inside any defined time or doing twenty push-ups. Many of the young men were in average to below average physical condition. The grinder separated the mentally and physical strong from the weak. I was not one of the weak recruits and performed on the

102

grinder with gusto and intention. In a strange way I looked forward to another hard day on the grinder.

One-Five Day

For the entire first week of basic training I kept hearing about "One-Five Day." I had no idea what a One-Five Day was, but I did have a strong feeling we were not going to bake cookies. I found out that on the fifth day of the first week as a valid company we were going to meet our first true test. We were to be inspected by one dozen company commanders to ensure everything was clean and in its place. There was considerable anxiety and worry throughout the company leading up to One-Five Day. I knew it was going to be a very long day but really didn't know what was in store for us. The not knowing part was the most mentally taxing component during our first week. In preparation of One-Five Day, I worked very hard at knowing key laws of the UCMJ by rote, ensuring my bunk and foot locker were in excellent shape, and preparing myself mentally for the inevitable unknown.

Immediately following breakfast on One-Five Day we mustered back at the barracks and were told to stand at attention in front of our bunks. A muster is a formal gathering to inspect and/or test military personnel. All of a sudden you could hear the stomp of boots coming up the staircase towards our third floor barracks. I immediately began focusing my full visual and mental attention on a single spot on a far wall and did not move until I was told to. There were company commanders swarming the entire barracks. They immediately began bearing down, screaming orders at any recruit they desired. I could hear

103

bunks and foot lockers being torn apart with recruits performing push-ups, body builders, and whatever else they were told to do. If any recruits were caught moving, looking around, or making a verbal mistake while reciting codes from the UCMJ, they were immediately verbally and physically abused. Knowing I was one of the leaders, I worked especially hard to ensure I didn't do something stupid or foolish. Unfortunately, it didn't go my way.

While at attention a female Company Commander stood in front of me and yelled out some off the cuff order. I instantaneously yelled out "Yes sir!!" The female company commander bellowed "Do I look like I have a pair of balls between my legs, recruit?" I yelled out "No ma'am" and began doing push-ups, body builders and running in place for the next hour or more. When the One-Five Day free for all was finished all of our clothing was piled in the middle of the barracks, the bunks were pushed back against the walls, and everyone was completely exhausted from extensive calisthenic exercises. To top it off, the barracks windows were closed and the place turned into a hot and nasty smelling sweat factory.

Punishments

There were many ways to punish those recruits that performed poorly with their studies, had bad attitudes about taking orders, or thought they were tougher than anyone else. The military has a way of producing agonizing mental and physical punishments that most normal people would never think about. Here are some punishments I witnessed being performed on the poor souls of some recruits.

The Pencil Screwing

This seemingly harmless form of physical punishment was reserved for recruits that performed poorly with their studies. The recruit was ordered to take a mechanical pencil and extract about one inch of lead from the writing tip. The recruit was ordered to stand at attention. With his arms stretched out in front of him, palms facing inward and his index fingers pointing straight out, the company commander would place the pencil between his index fingers. The intent was to maintain a hold on the pencil between the finger tips without breaking the lead. "Whatever you do, don't break the lead!" When your arms become unbearably heavy and the lead breaks then you start doing push-ups and body builders.

The Helicopter

The Helicopter was reserved for general stuff like failing to keep your boondockers spit shined or your clothes properly folded and stowed in your locker. The recruit was ordered to stand at attention then elevate his arms straight out from his sides, forming a T shape. The Company Commander then placed a boondocker on each hand. The intent was to hold onto the boondockers as long as you could. When your arms became unbearably heavy and you dropped either boot, you started doing push-ups and body builders.

Garbage Can Lovers

When you have eighty-three young men living together in a small space, stuff happens. There are those recruits that get caught grabbing and pinching each other, or snapping towels in the shower. I couldn't believe this next punishment until I witnessed it for myself.

Two recruits were caught by the Company Commander messing around and getting too playful with each other. They were doing the typical childhood stuff like pinching, grabbing and just acting quite childish and stupid. Each recruit was ordered to disrobe down to their underwear. One of the recruits was ordered to obtain the barracks trash can, empty it out on the floor and place it in the middle of the room. The two hundred and fifty gallon trash can was made of metal and could easily fit two people inside. All other recruits were told to stand at parade rest in front of their bunks. The two "playful" recruits were ordered to step inside the trash can facing each other. This meant they were nose to nose! The company commander then ordered each of them to yell as loud as they could "I love you." The two recruits yelled until they could no longer talk. The majority of other recruits (including myself) broke into gut splitting laughter and automatically went into doing push-ups and body builders.

Moture and Mini-Moture

There is always the recruit who thinks he doesn't have to take orders like everyone else. This is a recruit who thinks he is a big tough guy and can push people around. Either a full moture "motion torture" or mini-moture was in store for these recruits. A full moture was given to those recruits who completely disobeyed orders, got into fights or aggressively talked back to a Company Commander or his assistant. The gravity of the offense would make a difference upon how many days you would be subjected to moture. The full moture was for one full calendar week.

One of the recruits in our company thought he was a real tough guy. During a physical exercise session the commander got in his face and started screaming obscenities at him. The recruit punched the company commander sending him to the floor. The commander got up, said nothing, picked up his hat, straightened up his uniform and walked down stairs. Within a short couple of minutes you could hear the pounding of many boots coming up the stair case. In walked about six Navy Seals with a take-no- prisoner's attitude. They immediately secured the disobedient recruit and carried him out of the barracks. This recruit was absent from the company for an entire calendar week. His full moture consisted of doing calisthenic exercises, in full uniform, with his rifle for 45 minutes, given a 15 minute break then back to performing the exercises. He was constantly being harassed and yelled at by multiple company commanders during his moture. This was performed in and around the division sidewalk area which allowed everyone to hear the screaming and constant barrage of verbal obscenities. I don't recall how many hours each day the moture persisted, but it probably lasted until the recruit was near exhaustion. Needless to say, when this recruit was allowed back in the company he carried a much better attitude! A mini-moture was the same as the full moture except that its duration was three days or less. I didn't want anything to do with either of them and performed any order at any time to the best of my ability – no questions asked!

Division Sidewalk

There are recruits who think they are extremely squared away and believe they have their act together (me). Regardless of how well you perform, sooner or later you will screw up and pay the price. During a normal afternoon I was ordered by the company commander to march four recruits to the infirmary. I then ordered the recruits to muster outside in front of the barracks where I proceeded to march them across the basic training campus towards the infirmary. We reached the infirmary with no problems and after their appointments headed back to the barracks. During our march back, I was stopped by two Company Commanders. They began barking orders and demanded I show the correct paperwork that allowed us to be marching across the military base. Unfortunately, I left the paperwork back at the barracks. We were immediately marched over to our division sidewalk. Upon arrival, we were told to stand at attention and stay there until told otherwise. We stood at attention for one hour twenty-five minutes. My two main goals were to keep my mental focus and not allow myself to physically break down or pass out. During this timeframe three of the recruits either talked or moved inappropriately. Unknown to us, we were being watched the entire time. This meant the recruits that were busted from talking and moving had to stay behind for push-ups, body builders, and calisthenics, while the remainder of us marched back to the barracks. Upon our return to the barracks I was questioned by the other recruit petty officers why it took so long to get to and from the infirmary. I told them what happened and after they stopped laughing from my mistake, we went about our daily business.

RIF Phase Two

After two months of boot camp all the recruits in the company were broken out and assigned to various jobs to support the operations of the training facility. I was awarded the job as a RIF attendant. This was the same indoctrination facility I endured during my first three days of boot camp. It was now my turn to initially indoctrinate the incoming civilians into the Navy. As a co-leader of the company I knew all the protocols, rules and primary military laws. This allowed me and the other recruit leaders assigned to RIF to know our limits when mentally, physically and verbally pummeling the "fresh off the bus" civilians. We also knew the civilians had no idea who we were or what would face them on an hourly and daily basis. We definitely had the upper hand and were more than willing to dole out abuses with bravado and evil intentions. We were prepared to give similar or more abuses than those placed upon us when we entered the facility. Due to the inconsistent bus arrivals, our work schedule was erratic which kept our sleep to about four hours a night. The other RIF petty officers and I had so much fun verbally pummeling the civilians, sleep was an afterthought. However, after one full week of professional babysitting I was happy to be back with our original company.

New Orders

One week prior to graduation day, our next duty station orders were received by the division administration. During one typical weekday afternoon on the grinder, we were ordered to march back to the barracks earlier than normal so we could receive our next duty station assignments. This was a very exciting time for those recruits that passed the class room studies and physical training. Unfortunately a small percentage of recruits were either given general discharges or held back a few extra weeks from graduating. These special recruit cases were mostly from failing class room studies or the inability to swim. For those recruits that were scheduled to graduate, many of them were heading straight to the fleet somewhere in the world. It depended upon their job rating when they signed up. Other recruits were heading off to specialized training schools such as electronics, special forces, logistics or administration. Our RCPO was an ex-Ohio State Trooper. It was my understanding he had tested into the special forces program. I assumed he was going to San Diego, but didn't know for sure. When working with a local Navy recruiter each person is given the opportunity to either test into a specific field of work, or allowed to openly sign up. In both instances you were required to identify a maximum of four rates that were companion to your civilian capabilities. Depending upon how and what you tested in at the recruiting office would dictate which field of work you officially were assigned. For example, I tested successfully into the Advanced Electronics program and was allowed to pick my top four desired rates. I wanted to work as an electronics technician repairing and maintaining fighter jets. So my top pick was Aviation Electronics Technician.

Knowing I had passed the Advance Electronics test guaranteed my next assignment would be electronics school. I assumed I was going to work on fighter jets as an Aviation Electronics Technician. My assumption turned out to be incorrect. Upon receiving my orders I realized I was assigned as a Fire Control Technician. I assumed I was being placed on a team of firemen and believed my orders were incorrect. I asked our Company Commander about my new rate and he re-affirmed me it was a specialized rate, I would be heading off to electronics school and would learn about guided missile control systems. This was a grand relief to me but I still didn't know what type of missile system I would learn or the type of ship I would eventually call home.

Graduation Day

Each newly formed company starts with a single flag that has their company number on it. When marching with a single flag, all other companies could readily identify your company as the new recruits and would taunt us at every opportune moment. To earn additional flags the company must compete and excel in areas such as physical fitness, knowledge of the UCMJ and Navy, and of course marching in perfect unison. We quickly learned there was no "I" in teamwork and did everything we could to ensure our teammates excelled or passed every physical or scholastic exam. All competitions included every recruit in the company. For example, if the competition was running one mile, then the last person in the company across the finish line determined the final running time for the entire company. By graduation day our company had earned all but two flags.

Marching onto the athletic field during graduation day was an impressive site. Our company was well trained and ready to show off our military protocol better than any other company. There were multiple companies passing in review wearing full dress uniforms in

111

front of their families. Everyone was impressed at the razor sharp attentiveness toward military protocol. Prior to graduation day, all recruits were given customary graduation notices and invitations to mail out to their respective families and friends. Unfortunately for me, my invitations did not persuade family or friends to attend the ceremony. It was a proud day for me as a graduating Navy recruit, but a lonely and heart saddened day too. As a recruit leader I felt a little embarrassed that no one inside my family was attending the graduation. In a deep, yet profound, way I didn't expect my parents to attend. After all, my father had a history of not being on the sidelines during my high school football games or for anything related to track and field. Immediately after graduation, I found myself hanging out with a small number of other individual recruits and being introduced to other family attendees.

Thoughts for You

Basic training taught me when a real team works together, anything is possible. It also taught me more about myself as a beginning leader that I was capable of producing more than I expected. I experienced fear, uncertainty and doubt going into basic training but felt more like a leader upon graduation. All five of the slaughterhouse rules showed up in basic training, with some more significant than others. I was held *accountable* for teaching people how to march, even though I had never marched a step in my life. I maintained strong *integrity* through treating everyone equally and not showing favoritism to those who yearned for it. My *resilience* remained intact through long days of physical and mental challenges. I gained the *respect* of other recruit petty officers with my "can do" attitude coupled with mental and physical resilience. I very quickly learned to *respect* others in authoritative and leadership positions. And I learned to *trust* that my fellow recruits would perform to the best of their abilities.

I watched many young men mentally and physically suffer because they didn't show respect to authority figures. I experienced how some men fought against or didn't understand the true meaning of altruism as required with real team work. Basic training breaks down walls built of big egos, erases the race card, and ensures everyone has the opportunity to perform at his or her best.

Can you visualize yourself within the bubble of a Navy boot camp? Are you able to get along with your boss, peers, and subordinates while on the job or in private? Do you present a positive attitude with an open mind when meeting new people who are not like yourself? I believe everyone, including you, has the ability to openly excel as an individual and as part of a team. Everyone has some form of leadership qualities inside him or herself. Unfortunately, many people don't get a chance or opportunity to move themselves forward and experience those pent-up leadership qualities. When given the opportunity to make a positive change, no matter how big or small, don't forget to pick up that challenging fork in the road. You may be surprised by what you might learn about yourself once you commit to walking through a door not knowing what is on the other side.

*****

"Everything you've ever wanted is on the other side of fear." George Addair

Chapter 8 - Military School

Navy Base and Barracks Living

Immediately after graduation my new duty station was the Great Lakes Naval Training Center, located north of Chicago, Illinois. For me this new duty station was good and bad. On the good side, my home town was one hundred-fifty miles west of the Navy base which made earned weekend visits a possibility. On the bad side, I knew I would be putting up with the elements of a northern Illinois winter.

While living in the school barracks each sailor was assigned a duty section. This meant doing assigned duty inside and outside the barracks. Standing watch while on duty was mandatory with watch stations lasting between two to four hours. The duty watches would start immediately after school and end at 0600 hours the following morning. An example of a standard "clean" duty watch would be managing, guiding and directing personnel coming in and going out through the front door of the school barracks. This included maintaining the entrance and exit log. The sailor on duty was responsible to keep an active log of everyone that enters or leaves the barracks. Another example would be standing guard outdoors as the front door sentry, or performing a roving watch outside and around the barracks. Any watch duty stationed outside the barracks in the dead of winter was not enjoyable. The humid bitter cold blowing in from Lake Michigan was not something I was looking forward to. To withstand outside watch duty during the winter months, I ensured I had plenty of extra winter clothing to wear beneath my Navy uniform. It was a constant battle to stay warm.

115

For many months the new students were not allowed to leave the Navy base. It was a privilege to leave the base and the privilege had to be earned. This worked well for me as I was working myself out of financial debt and had to spend as little as possible. For the first three months I didn't leave the Navy base whether I had liberty or not. Navy liberty is defined as regular time off on weekends or holidays but not to exceed seventy-two hours. Instead, I would eat at the enlisted men's mess hall, have a beer or two a week at the enlisted men's club, play some pool, or hang out in the barracks reading a book I had checked out from the library. There was rotating cleaning duty which meant scrubbing toilets and cleaning the restrooms (heads). I kept myself out of trouble, my uniform in excellent condition, and our room as clean as possible.

My life was narrowed to spending a lot of time on base and spending very little money. I committed myself to living on twenty dollars a month. All the rest of my earned pay went to paying off any financial debts left behind prior to joining. At the end of six months I was debt free. The only outstanding monthly payment I had was child support payments that were automatically paid to the circuit court. I happily paid the child support payments as I believed I was accountable for bringing a new life into the world. I also felt and believed my personal integrity would be challenged if I didn't step up and make the expected support payments. Besides, these payments were for the ongoing support of our daughter, whom I missed and loved dearly.

Assistant Platoon Leader

One day while standing alongside a small group of students in the common area of the barracks, I listened to the current Assistant Platoon Leader complain about his duties and how they interfered with his liberty away from the barracks and the base. I could tell he did not desire this position and was looking for an excuse not to perform his duty as the Assistant Platoon Leader. I made a deal with him saying I would perform his duties while the Platoon Leader was away for the weekend. He agreed and suddenly I was walking around with a clipboard in my hands telling people what to do and when to do it. During muster on Monday morning the Assistant Platoon Leader and I approached our Platoon Leader with the agreed arrangement. From that point forward I became the Assistant Platoon Leader. My new role was to muster the men before and after school, ensure all the barracks chores and duty watches were accomplished on time and in high quality. Plus it was my responsibility to help ensure everyone in the platoon was abiding by the UCMJ. My new leadership position was not a popular role. However, as the Assistant Platoon Leader, I no longer had to clean floors and scrub toilets!

NEET School

I was assigned to a barracks that contained sailors attending the Navy Electricity and Electronics Training (NEET) School. In the student barracks there were four sailors assigned to each room. NEET is comprised of twenty-four individual modules with each module covering a different topic in either electrical or electronics. Each module had a time stamp assigned to it. Meaning, each student had a pre-defined number of hours and minutes to complete studying for the module, take a test and pass accordingly. As you advanced through the modules they became more advanced and more time was given to completion. Some modules included a physical lab which had to be passed in conjunction with the written test. The NEET School dropout rate consistently hovered around forty percent. If the student failed either a written or physical lab test within a module this was considered as strike one. The student was then given two more opportunities to pass the module test. After three strikes within the same module he was kicked out of the program and immediately sent to the fleet. When sent to the fleet without any advanced training, the sailor would most likely be assigned the rate of Boatswain Mate. The Boatswain Mate job is highly regarded as "Everything fundamental Navy" but a job that I didn't care to employ, nor did it fit into my ten year plan.

During the course work I succeeded with flying colors to pass all modules until I got to module nineteen. I experienced my first test failure and was given a written notice that was placed in my school record. I subsequently became more focused during my studies and passed module nineteen. However, I ran into a virtual chain saw during module twenty-three. During my studies with module twenty-three, I successively failed the lab test twice. After the second failure I was ordered to report to the Executive Officers' office and explain why my head was not in the game. The Executive Officer got in my face and told me that if I didn't pass the lab on my third attempt, I would be dropped from the school and immediately shipped out to the fleet.

The NEET School had its own library system where sailors could peacefully study. Knowing my entire future Navy career was on the line, I planted myself in this library until I practically memorized all the lab material and its known test points and nomenclature. When I had one hour left on the clock, I went back into the lab where I successfully passed the test. A huge weight was lifted off my shoulders and with great relief I prepared myself for the final module.

Late

During my tenure at NEET School I earned off-base privileges on any weekends that I didn't have duty. I convinced a friend of mine back home to drive out to Chicago, pick me up and drive me back so I could get my pickup truck. Having off-base privileges plus owning a vehicle made me a popular sailor in the barracks. On occasions, a few of us sailors would travel up to Milwaukee and hit the clubs on Friday or Saturday nights. The majority of my liberty weekends were spent back home, with attempts to visit my daughter and hang out with friends. During one of my weekend outings at home, I decided to drive back to Chicago leaving town at 03:00 hours Monday morning. I had to be back to the Navy base prior to 07:00 hours and muster my platoon at 07:45 hours before school started. I knew it was a full three hour drive to get back to the base and gave myself an extra hour due to Chicago traffic.

Through the overnight Chicago had experienced heavy rains, local flooding and some high winds. Upon my arrival into the Chicago freeway toll system, the traffic was at a standstill. I had miscalculated the excessive delay time and ended up two hours late returning to my barracks. Early morning muster had already taken place, school was in session and I was considered as Absent Without Leave (AWOL). I knew I was in deep hot water! Upon arrival to the barracks I went straight to the school's division office in preparation of receiving my punishment. The officer on duty was really angry at me not for just being late, but because I was the Assistant Platoon Leader. He immediately gave me thirty days restriction to the base and thirty days extra duty. I didn't mind the thirty days restriction to the base but the extra duty was something I was not looking forward to.

My extra duty was the outdoor roving patrol watch around the base every night as directed by the officer in charge. This meant walking around the base in between buildings from either 20:00 to 00:00 or 00:00 to 04:00 hours as the security patrol. It was late winter and the weather outside was very unpredictable. There were many long cold nights on patrol when I felt wet and cold to the bone. I did however, use the restriction to the base to focus my energy to successfully pass Module 24 and graduate from NEET School. Unfortunately for me, my tardiness cost me some respect and trust from our school's division officer. It was a hard lesson and a reminder about why the slaughterhouse rules should and must be adhered to at all times.

Navy "A" School

Immediately after NEET School I received orders to attend my next school entitled "A" School. I was moved into different barracks with a new set of roommates. The A School was an advanced technical school with both written instruction and physical labs. Class time started at 08:00 hours and went until 16:00 hours each day. The course work was broken out into sections, and we were quizzed on content daily. We were given an exam every Friday afternoon. Everyone was expected and required to pass every quiz and exam. Mandatory study was given to anyone who failed a quiz, an exam or showed up late for any class at any time. If the sailor did well in class, kept his uniform in top condition, maintained his room and passed the three times per week room inspections, he was granted volunteer study. Every entitlement had to be earned. There was nothing given. Depending upon how well each sailor performed in A School would dictate the amount and level of restrictions he had to live under. If he excelled in his studies and kept himself out of trouble then the restrictions would ease accordingly. Since I was the Assistant Platoon Leader during NEET School, I was assigned as Class Leader in my A School. Once again I cherished being given a leadership position. As Class Leader I gained the respect of the other students and my Platoon Leader. The days of anger, internal rage and frustration were in the rear-view mirror. My new position instilled a stronger sense in definiteness of purpose within me.

The Offer

Everything was going quite well for me during my A School tenure. I had excellent grades, didn't break any Navy base rules and re-earned my off base privileges. If I didn't have weekend duty I was allowed to drive home, spend time with friends and work at visiting my daughter. My ex-wife was still leveraging our daughter against me. Leverage consisted of asking for more money if I wanted to spend time with our daughter. Sometimes I got lucky to see her for a Saturday or Sunday afternoon. Sometimes I didn't get to see her at all.

The A School curriculum was broken out into three different phases. We were required to pass and graduate from each phase. At the end of phase three there was a small ceremony for the graduating class. After graduation we were then assigned a new duty station so we could attend our "C" School. C School was a specialized training school dedicated to a specific gun and missile fire control system. Since I was an FTM E3 (Fire Control Technician - Missiles Enlisted rank of three), I would be assigned to learn a specific missile control system. In the early nineteen eighties, the most common missile systems aboard ship were Tarter and Harpoon. To learn either of these systems in the respective C School would take an additional one full year of training and then you would be sent to the fleet. Since I had tested into the Advanced Electronics Field, I was expecting my collective training time for boot camp, NEET School, A school and C school to be two and one-half years. Then it was three and one-half more years serving on a Navy ship.

Mid-way through phase three of my A School, I was ordered to the Executive Officers office again. I had no idea why I was being ordered to this man's office and was quite puzzled about the order. Many of my student comrades quickly heard about the bewildering ordeal of their Class Leader and Assistant Platoon Leader. I presented myself to the Executive Officer on time and with military pride and conviction. I was told to relax and stand at parade rest while the Executive Officer presented me an optional set of new orders. Instead of going to my C School I was being offered a permanent change of duty station for one year, located on the west coast. The duty station was at the Naval Ship Weapon Systems Engineering Station – NSWSES. Think of NSWSES as the Pentagon of the West Coast. This tightly controlled government engineering directorate is located fifty miles northwest of Los Angeles (L.A.) in Port Hueneme, California. Today the engineering directorate is entitled "Naval Service Warfare Center." The orders stated this one year of duty was classified as neutral duty which didn't count against any future earned shore duty or sea time. The orders also stated I would not receive my C School, and my Navy service was shortened from six active service years to four years. I was told that two sailors were picked out of the school for this special neutral duty and I was one of them. The orders were strictly voluntary and I had twenty-four hours to think about my decision. This new opportunity was a curve ball to my ten year plan! At this point I was completely confused about these new orders and didn't know what to do because I was already psychologically committed to my six year contract. Plus, I was looking forward to my C School.

Upon my return to the barracks I was immediately ordered to the Platoon Leader's office to explain the meeting I had with the Executive Officer. Our Platoon Leader was a First Class Petty Officer and this was his earned shore duty station. In the Navy you have to earn your shore duty by spending "X" number of years aboard ship. The type of job you held would dictate your sea/shore rotation schedule. As a Fire Control Technician our sea/shore rotation schedule was set at three and one-half years of sea time then two and one-half years of shore duty. The Platoon Leader grilled me about the meeting with our Executive Officer and I told him the details. To my surprise our Platoon Leader was from Port Hueneme and knew everything about the engineering directorate! He convinced me that I was a very lucky man and this was an opportunity of a lifetime. Apparently, this particular command is given to those officers that are exemplary, officers on their final tour of duty or senior enlisted personnel just prior to military retirement. To have the opportunity to serve at NSWS was truly extraordinary for an FTM E-3 Fire Control Technician. I was in the right place at the right time! The very next day I met with the Executive Officer and told him I accepted the new orders. Once again I came to a fork in the road. I picked up the fork, put it in my pocket and walked through a door not exactly knowing what was on the other side.

Thoughts for You

The slaughterhouse rules served me well during my tenure as a military student. Through my resilience in self-study I was able to pass all the modules in NEET School and graduate. Because of my platoon and school leadership positions, I was held accountable for the outcomes of other's while expected to maintain a high level of personal integrity. Accepting increased accountability while building trust with my superiors positioned me as a candidate into a west coast engineering directorate I didn't know existed.

Since my Navy years I have told this story to various friends and family and openly stated how lucky I was - being at the right place at the right time. Looking back on this experience I believe it's not entirely about luck. It's also about stepping up to accountability, maintaining personal integrity, leveraging resilience from within, building mutual respect with people and building trusted working relationships. It's about willingly putting your best self forward in different situations and living by the slaughterhouse rules.

*****

"Definiteness of purpose is the starting point of all achievement." W. Clement Stone

Chapter 9 - California or Bust

The New Duty Station

When I accepted the new orders I automatically received thirty days paid leave due to a permanent change of duty stations. In other words, the Navy gave me thirty days to move. I added another two weeks of earned paid leave so my total time to get my butt to California was forty-five days. Most of my paid leave time was spent back at my home town visiting a few "solid" friends, visiting family members, and spending as much negotiated time as I could with my daughter. I gave myself one full week to drive to California. Along the way I stopped off in Omaha to visit with an aunt and uncle then stopped in Las Vegas for a couple of nights on the town. The driving trip was quite enjoyable and I arrived at the front gate of the Port Hueneme Naval Base with my new orders on time and eager to get to work. However, I had no idea what I would be doing for work or duty.

Barracks Living

I was assigned to one of the base barracks and shared a room with a Navy Seal who was working as an underwater demolition expert. Every morning my roommate would jump out of his bunk and start doing push-ups in his underwear. The guy was exceptionally physically fit and would do at least one-hundred push-ups just to start his day. I would put on my running gear and run three to five miles every morning. I respected his ability to do push-ups and he respected my ability to run five minute miles. We became good roommates and gained mutual respect for each other's physical abilities.

The barracks was filled with young Seabees working their way through Seabee training and other technical schools. A Seabee is a member of the Navy's construction forces. The word "Seabee" comes from initials "CB", which in turn comes from the term "Construction Battalion." I was only one of two Fire Control Technicians living inside the base barracks. My normal work days were different from the Seabees and when I wore my dress uniform, I got plenty of odd looks and questions. This was because the Navy dress uniform would display the sailor's rate and rank. My rate was outside the local element of Navy Seabees, hence the questions and different looks. I enjoyed hanging out with the student Seabees and learning more about a function of the Navy I didn't know existed. All was good with barracks living at my new duty station.

NSWSES

The engineering directorate's purpose was to test, evaluate and provide integrated logistics support for surface warfare combat and weapon systems. The engineering directorate had approximately one thousand two hundred fifty civilian government employees (civil servants) and approximately sixty-five active duty Navy personnel. The non-officer Navy personnel consisted of one Senior Chief Petty Officer (E-8), one Chief Petty Officer (E-7) two First Class Petty Officers (E-6's), one Third Class Petty Officer (E-4) and two Seamen (E-3). I was one of the two Seamen. All other personnel were Naval Officers ranking between Lieutenant Junior Grade (O-2) through Captain (O-6). With a small ratio of active duty personnel to civil servants the strict military protocol between active duty enlisted and officers was quite lax and open. For example, while passing an officer between buildings and passageways, it was customary to salute at every exchange. Since I had just left a very strict military school I always saluted the officers until told otherwise. As an enlisted service man it was important to me that I show complete respect with military rank to the officers. For the entire year at this new duty station I was repeatedly told by various officers that I didn't have to salute - I saluted anyway. I knew after my one year tenure at NSWES I would be assigned to a fleet warship, which would require full military protocol. As an active duty enlisted military man I had worked diligently with upholding the slaughterhouse rules and I wanted to extend this work effort to my future fleet command.

Missile Test Site and Computer Technician

My first assigned position was to maintain and help manage a missile test site located at the far southwest corner of the Navy base. This missile test site was operated by two First Class Petty Officers. As a Navy Seamen assigned to the test site, the majority of the work was basic cleaning and running missile test launch orders as directed by the engineering directorate. Once tests were performed the test report was handed over to the directorate's officers and then communicated back to the Pentagon. Most of my free time at the test site was dedicated to reading and learning about the missile test system and maintaining the security and overall working capabilities of the test site property. The work was not demanding nor overly challenging, so I decided to work with our Senior Chief Petty Officer and see what other opportunities were available. Showing the eagerness to learn while maintaining accountability with my current duties got me a new assignment.

The new assignment consisted of maintaining computers and peripherals, running diagnostic test programs and fixing computer and networking problems in an advanced software lab. The lab was located on base and consisted of a raised floor computing environment located in a tightly secured building. The building housing the computer facility was surrounded by tall fencing with razor wire across the top. Access was restricted to those military and civil service personnel with the need to know, correct paperwork and electronic badge access. During a normal workday, there were forty to fifty programmers in the building writing and testing software code for the new Tomahawk Cruise Missile system. A key deployment of this system was targeted for the USS New Jersey – one of the WWII battleships being refurbished and outfitted with the latest weaponry. As a lab technician my main responsibilities were to ensure the computers and peripheral systems were up and running so the new programming code could be effectively tested before it was loaded into the Tomahawk missile test system located at an adjoining Navy base. If you have ever seen an earlier James Bond movie there are scenes that depict computing rooms housing rotating vertical discs on computing machines with technicians wearing white lab coats. My environment was very similar looking to the scene out of a James Bond movie. I was one of the technicians wearing a white lab coat with a badge clipped to the lapel. It was a very different working environment and culture than working in a slaughterhouse!

Military Duty

The software test lab was my day job that felt much more like any civilian nine to five position. Once a month for an entire week I had military duty. This duty consisted of being the duty driver for all officers stationed to the base and officers or political dignitaries visiting from other military bases or government installations. My primary driving duty was driving officers to/from L.A. International Airport (LAX). I was given the keys to the motor pool and a pager (the latest and greatest mobile technology). Anytime I was paged I would call the number listed and receive orders of who to pick up, where and when. The automobile I drove was a four door sedan with all black interior and exterior. It sported basic tires with small chrome hub caps. It was a very basic automobile that was easy to spot as a government owned vehicle. I always drove with the lights on and when picking up dignitaries, the vehicle was dressed with a United States flag on each end of the front bumper. There was strict military protocol I had to learn and adhere to while transporting officers and dignitaries to or from any location. For example, I would pop to attention and greet each officer or dignitary with a military salute. While waiting curbside I would stand at parade rest next to the driver's door. This was especially interesting when waiting curbside at LAX. People would approach me and ask specific questions about the Navy, inquire about military service or ask questions about what I was doing and why. I had to memorize each officer's name, rank, and any other pertinent information given to me to ensure protocol was maintained. My dress uniform had to be spotless, pressed to meet military standards, and always ready at a moment's notice.

The Officers' Ball Incident

The annual Officers Ball was scheduled during my assigned week of duty driving. It was a perfect weather weekend and all the officers assigned to the directorate were prepping and readying themselves for Saturday night's ball. Each year the Officers Ball was hosted at the Bard Mansion located in the Southeast portion of the Navy base. As the duty driver it was my job to pick up the Navy base Captain, his wife, plus any visiting Washington dignitaries on the invitation list and drive them to and from the ball. Everything was going as planned. I made multiple trips and dropped off the assigned officers and their wives. I drove the car back to the barracks and waited to receive a page instructing me to pick up the Navy base captain and his wife. At about 22:00 hours I drove to the Officers' Ball, parked the car directly in front of the building, opened the doors then stood at parade rest waiting for the captain and his wife to appear. I had been waiting for at least twenty minutes when suddenly a Marine Corps Major, adorned in his full dress white uniform with saber, approached me. The Major said "Good evening Seaman Myers" and then walked away. Like a mindless toad I said "Good evening sir," and did not pop to attention or salute and address the Major accordingly. The major walked about two steps away, turned around, jumped in front of me, and started yelling at me (in front of his wife) about military protocol. He berated me until he believed I knew I had screwed up and ensured I wouldn't make the mistake again.

From that moment forward I never made another military protocol mistake!

A New Relationship

Shortly after arriving at NSWSES I noticed a beautiful young brunette woman working as an administrative assistant in the directorate. Over a period of a few weeks, I opened up multiple conversations with her. Our small talk turned into me convincing her to go out on a date. One date turned into many dates and we started to become intimately entangled within each other's lives. As the weeks and months passed, it became very apparent we were falling in love. However, we both knew I was on a temporary one year assignment and my next duty station would be somewhere in the fleet. We openly talked about our predicament and were uncertain what the future held for our relationship. I told her about my ten year plan and how I wanted my future to be in engineering. Nothing was left on the table about our pasts and future dreams. With a warm heart and a strong desire to share my life with her, I asked her to marry me. She said "yes." We were now an engaged couple with an unknown future living situation. We did know the love for each other was real and agreed we would develop a plan about managing our relationship when the time approached. Hey wait a minute. This was not part of my ten year plan! It's great to have a plan and to accept that sometimes plans change.

Advancement

As an E-3 Navy Seamen I was eager to earn and be promoted to the rank of Third Class Petty Officer as soon as practicable. The Navy

132

has very specific requirements to qualify for any promotion. During my west coast tenure I worked diligently on acquiring all the necessary requirements to be promoted to Petty Officer Third Class. I had excelled as a military student and accepted leadership roles in two prior schools. I learned and supported executive military protocol as a duty driver and I had diligently studied and prepared myself to take and pass the Petty Officer Third Class exam. I passed the exam; and prior to ending my one year tenure at the engineering directorate, I was promoted accordingly. This promotion was very important to me because I knew that going to the fleet as a Petty Officer in a highly technical job would help ensure I was assigned to a leading edge missile system. I was now ready to be transferred to the fleet as an official Petty Officer Third Class.

Thoughts for You

I made the most of my tenure at the west coast engineering directorate. I worked hard to learn Navy protocol while on duty as a duty driver. I learned as much as I could as a computer lab technician. I enjoyed having the opportunity to build trusted relationships with officers and higher ranking enlisted Petty Officers. During my free time I enrolled into night school at a local community college and took an English communications class. My new found relationship and the love I had for a local woman filled my heart with joy. The slaughterhouse rules seemed to harmonize with my new military life.

Looking back on that one single year in my life I realize it was a year of personal and professional growth, and opportunity. It was a defining year for my military service and the beginning of a new-found long lasting personal relationship. Can you identify any particular year or time period in your life that presented itself with significant changes – either positive or negative? Within that time period can you identify which personal and/or professional connections supported your desires, dreams and wishes for the future? I believe that upholding the slaughterhouse rules to the best of one's ability can create a solid base for propelling one's self toward a more rewarding personal and professional future. For me, the year at the engineering directorate, finding new love and living by the slaughterhouse rules was a beginning cornerstone that supported the remaining Navy years ahead.

*****

"I am not a product of my circumstances. I am a product of my decisions." Stephen Covey

Chapter 10 - Off to the Fleet

The Real Navy

While stationed at the engineering directorate I formed a trusting relationship with a Navy Captain who helped me obtain my next duty station. Instead of being told where and when I was going, I was given three options that were all fleet bound but in different ports on different types of ships. My options for ships were Destroyer, Cruiser, or Frigate. The assigned ports for each type of ship were Pearl Harbor, Hawaii; San Diego, California; and Mayport, Florida respectively. I selected the USS Gallery, FFG-26. This was a brand new Guided Missile Frigate – an Oliver Hazard Perry class ship built and currently stationed at the time in Bath Iron Works, Bath, Maine. The ship's designated home port was Mayport, Florida. I picked the ship because it was new to the fleet, supported a new type of missile system and its home port of Mayport gave me the potential opportunity to visit my daughter during extended periods of in-port earned leave time. Having a choice of your next duty station was unheard of for a Third Class Petty Officer. I knew I was in a very fortunate position and appreciated the opportunity provided to me by my Navy Captain friend and confidant.

Just prior to leaving the engineering directorate, I was briefed about the ship through my Navy Captain friend. He told me to assimilate myself as quickly as possible with the ship's crew, keep focused on my work and expect to become deeply integrated into a higher sense of team work than I had ever experienced. I was eager to step onboard the ship and begin experiencing the real Navy.

A Surprise Set of Tech School Orders

The move from the west coast to the USS Gallery was considered a permanent change of duty station. Because it was a permanent move I received thirty days of paid leave to move myself from Port Hueneme, California to Mayport, Florida by way of Bath, Maine. This paid leave gave me time to drive back to northern Illinois and spend a couple weeks visiting my daughter, family and friends. During my paid leave time I was surprised to receive a new set of temporary orders. I was to report to a tightly controlled military computer repair school in Dam Neck, Virginia. Apparently, the Gallery required two computer repair technicians and I filled the second position. After just a week at home I loaded up my sea bag and drove myself to Virginia.

I spent the next four weeks learning how to repair printed circuit boards. Our final exam lasted one full work week. The instructor handed each student a printed circuit board that was split in half. Our job was to repair and rebuild the board with its components back to its original condition. I successfully passed the test and was awarded as a Certified Micro-Miniature Repair Technician. Immediately after graduation I drove back to Northern Illinois. Back at home I had three more weeks of leave time. Within this time period I had to drive to Mayport, store my car in temporary on-base storage, fly to Bath Main and report to the ship on time.

Bath Iron Works

I spent two months in Bath, Maine and fully enjoyed getting to know the layout of the ship, my position in the weapons systems division, my ship mates and of course the local lobster cuisine. An awesome shipyard in size, the Bath shipyard was home to the second largest crane in the world. A crane large enough it could pick up a completed section of a ship while gently maneuvering it into place for final construction. The USS Gallery was in its final preparations before going out to sea and testing its end-to-end operational functionality.

The ship's first assignment was a sea trial just off the coast of Maine via the Kennebec River. I assumed the sea trial was to ensure the ship could perform its functional capabilities and to ensure it wouldn't sink! After the sea trial we left Bath Iron Works and headed straight to our designated home port of Mayport, Florida. The Port of Mayport is located just east of Jacksonville, Florida and hosts a number of Navy warships and other complementary support vessels.

Gitmo

During my two month tenure at Bath, Maine my new found love in California was preparing to move across the country and meet me in Jacksonville. We both decided it was better for her to move to Jacksonville and find a job as an administrative assistant while I actively served in the Navy. When the ship was in port, we could spend time together and work on building our future relationship. She found an apartment on the northeast side of Jacksonville, and when my ship arrived in Mayport, we finished moving into our new apartment home.

While in Mayport the crew began prepping the ship for its first Refresher Training (Reftra) in Guantanamo Bay (Gitmo), Cuba. All new ships immediately go to Gitmo for an extensive six to eight week training period with multiple system shake down exercises. Then, every eighteen months after the first refresher training the ship and its crew are scheduled for Reftra again. Due to crew turnover, Reftras are critical to keep Navy crews knowledgeable and ready to perform in any type of military conflagration. During my tour on the Gallery, I experienced two Reftra assignments in Gitmo. My total time spent in Gitmo over the course of two refresher trainings was about four months.

The working days in and around the port of Gitmo were comprised of very long working hours. The weather outside was mostly hot and humid. Each day the ship's crew was ordered to cruise out to a specified area in the Caribbean Sea for testing. Testing and scoring was performed by certified Navy auditors whose full time job was to find excuses not to pass you on any given test. On a per division basis, the auditors would walk around with clip boards and look over your shoulder when performing on-the-job assessments. All systems, processes and technologies integrated to the ship had to be tested and re-tested until a passing grade was achieved. Each division had their own procedures and tests. Our weapons division was tested on system readiness, including operational processes for target acquisition, weapon launches and anything related to managing and operating the gun and missile fire control system. This included situations while in home port, cruising in hostile waters or during battle stations. Since the ship was new with a rookie crew there was zero leeway given to any minor mistakes. We were tested and re-tested again and again until we could prove to the auditors each job function could be performed with top precision. To pass every test meant you had to earn it. Nothing was given.

The Tear Gas Chamber

While in port there were various operational tests given on base. One of the tests was the tear gas chamber test. This was a test that everyone dreaded. All of us sailors also experienced the tear gas chamber test while in boot camp, so this was our second time around. The tear gas chamber was built out of a stationary semi-trailer. Small groups of sailors would enter the trailer with their gas masks stowed in their side pouches until told otherwise. The officer in charge was wearing a full anti-gas suit with a breathing apparatus, but all we had was our crappy gas masks. The officer would drop pellets into a bucket of water that immediately created a tear gas cloud. Our test consisted of breathing in the tear gas, then upon order pulling the mask out of its pouch, putting it on, clearing any gas in the mask then stating your name, rank and serial number when called upon. Of course, everyone suffered from breathing excessive tear gas. The gas was so strong some guys would vomit while the rest of us suffered through shortness of breath, uncontrollable tears, and runny noses. It was most definitely not a fun time but a great way to clear your sinuses!

DesRon 8 & Competition

Our ship was assigned to Destroyer Squadron Eight (DesRon 8). All similar warships within the squadron compete against each other during Reftra. Think of it as the Navy ship Olympics where competition breeds best in class. Competition is framed on a per division basis between similar ships. Our weapons division took top honors in most, but not all, of the competitive tests. When you see a Navy ship sporting various flags, these flags represent which ship is the best at what they do on a per division basis. There is tremendous pride when pulling into any port showing off your earned flags.

Liberty in Gitmo

Gitmo was not the best place to enjoy liberty. There were a few local on-base bars where all of us sailors would spend some free time drinking a beer or two – ok, lots of beers! This included any Marines assigned to the base. There were multiple opportunities for Marines and Sailors to butt heads. A few fists flew every now and then, but nothing too crazy. If we had enough liberty time, there were softball fields, basketball and tennis courts nearby. The Navy base operated a small sports equipment facility where you could check out equipment for sports play. There was also a small dock area where you could check out Hobie Cats, canoes and other small sailing craft for some leisure time out in the bay.

Prior to leaving home port some of the ship's crew pulled together volunteer money to purchase fishing tackle. Whenever time was allocated and available you could always find a sailor or two fishing off the fantail of the ship while in port at Gitmo. In one fishing occasion, a crew member caught a three to four foot shark using a hotdog as bait while fishing off the ship's main deck. One of the cooks eagerly apprehended the shark and in a short time he was sharing shark steaks with various crew members. At the end of the day, we all worked together and supported each other as military servicemen. After two months of testing and training out of Gitmo, it was time to head back to Mayport and prepare for our first fleet assignment.

All the Hot Zones

During the two years I lived and worked on the USS Gallery, we were appointed to many new assignments. Most assignments are outside the writing intent of this book. There were however, two assignments that impacted me the most. Those two assignments were the Pacific Station and the Mediterranean Cruise (Med Cruise).

Pacific Station

During a weekday while the ship was home ported in Mayport, I received an evening phone call from our First Class Petty Officer in Weapons Division. I was told that we would be shipping out in two weeks and I had to have all my personal finances in order including my last will and testament completed. I was not told where we were going, how long we would be gone or why. At the time my girlfriend and I were sharing a small one bedroom apartment in Jacksonville. Our plan was to marry once my tour of duty ended. However, learning about the new orders created a sense of urgency to marry. As an unmarried couple, if anything life-ending happened to me, my girlfriend would get nothing from my sacrifice. We decided to hire a justice of the peace and get married in our living room as soon as possible. The ship's photographer would manage picture taking and we asked another married couple from the ship to be our witnesses. Within one week we were married then managed to squeeze in a brief two-day honeymoon at Disney World in Orlando, Florida.

Giving Back - One

Right at the two week mark we shipped out and headed south from Mayport toward the Caribbean Sea. When the ship was underway at sea, the captain commandeered the ship's internal communication system and told us we were heading to a duty station off the west coast of Nicaragua. At the time Nicaragua was considered a hot zone of activity due to the revolution between the country's Contras (a rightist collection of counter-revolutionary groups) and Sandinistas (a leftist collection of political parties). In the early 1980s it was entitled the Contra War. Luckily for the USS Gallery, we were going to experience navigating the Panama Canal.

Prior to arriving at the Panama Canal, we stopped at an unknown town called Tela, Honduras, for goodwill purposes. Tela is a very small port town and the local Red Cross was in need of some good hands on labor. The ships crew volunteered to perform work activities such as building walls, painting, repairing electrical and plumbing utilities and cleaning streets. Just about anything we could do to help with the local infrastructure and make the Tela residents' lives better lived. The town's people were very poor and you could see misery in the streets. For example, every evening mother's would dress their daughters in their best dresses, then escort them down to the pier in hopes of getting them married to a U.S. Sailor. Of course, wedding ceremonies never happened. We also had to have the pier's garbage dumpster under military guard to ensure local men wouldn't fight over our food waste products. Every evening I witnessed dozens of young boys and girls lined up side-by-side on the wooden pier trying to snag a small fish using a piece of string with a hook attached. If a fish was caught they would pull a small wooden stick out of their pocket and immediately de-scale the fish then eat it on the spot – that was their dinner and most likely the only source of daily nutrition. The crew spent three days in Tela helping the local Red Cross and then it was off to transiting the Panama Canal.

Panama Canal

Our next international experience was making it through the Panama Canal. As a United States military vessel we were given priority status and placed first in line to transit the canal. Our transit date was May 20, 1983. It was truly a wonderful learning experience watching the intricate operations of the canal. After we transited the canal we ported in Panama City, Panama. During our time ported in Panama City we picked up a small group of Marines and from what I could surmise, another small group of men from the CIA. We took on fuel and food and headed north to the Pacific Ocean coastal waters off Nicaragua.

Our duty off the coast of Nicaragua was to track and record all air traffic going in and out of Managua, the country's capital city, plus any identified sea-faring traffic up and down the coast. Data collection was every day whereas uploading the stored data was performed at night while in communication with a military aircraft many miles out into international waters. The ship's geographic cruising and search area was small. This meant cruising within the same geographic area every day for thirty consecutive days. The days were long and boring, the weather hot and humid. To pass free time one of the ship's officers had an idea to facilitate an on-board Olympics. Our Olympic games were entitled "The Deranged Olympics." Competition was between the various divisions that made up the ship's crew. Here are a few examples of our deranged competitions:

- Spitting contest. One sailor was picked from each division to compete. To win the spit spot had to be the size of a quarter or larger. I won this contest with a spit length of twenty-six feet.

- Water drinking. Three sailors from each division competed to see how fast they could drink three gallons of water in consecutive order.

- Head stands. One person was picked from each division to see who could maintain a three-point head stand the longest.

I guess when you spend long boring days at sea with a large group of sailors, creativity with activity helps to keep everyone's spirits up. At the end of each thirty day cycle we would cruise back to Panama City for re-fueling and food stores. Our liberty was set at three days and it was back to our duty station off the Nicaraguan coast. This rotation went on for three months until we were relieved by another US Navy warship.

Pollywog to Shellback

During our final journey back to Panama City the entire ship's crew were given two choices; liberty in Acapulco, Mexico, or no liberty and keep cruising south to cross the equatorial line and go through shellback initiation. The ship's crew voted and we ended up crossing the equatorial line, then living through two days of initiation and earning our shellback designation. When a Navy ship crosses the equatorial line all designated pollywogs (non-shellbacks) had to endure a shellback initiation. All Navy personnel identified and proven to be shellbacks created and hosted the initiation and ceremony. Becoming a shellback in the US Navy is a very long-standing time honored tradition and is held for only the most seaworthy salts of the seas. For an understanding and description of what becoming a shellback means, the following was excerpted from the Veterans United Network website: https://www.veteransunited.com/network/the-navys-line-crossing-ceremony-revealed/

"The Navy is chock full of myth and tradition, and what happens at sea even affects our language. Many naval traditions, from the Sirens and Sea Monsters of the Odyssey to the boatswain's call, date back hundreds and even thousands of years. The Line Crossing Ceremony might just be the most interesting of today's naval traditions. Line crossing ceremonies have been a part of the western seafaring naval tradition for at least four hundred years. No one is really sure when or how the Line Crossing Ceremony, "Order of Neptune", came about. The ceremony observes a mariner's transformation from slimy Pollywog, a seaman who hasn't crossed the equator, to trusty Shellback, also called a Son or Daughter of Neptune. It was a way for sailors to be tested for their seaworthiness. When a ship crosses the equator, King Neptune comes aboard to exercise authority over his domain and to judge charges brought against Pollywogs that they are only posing as sailors and haven't paid proper homage to the god of the sea. High-ranking members of the crew and those who have been Shellbacks the longest dress up in elaborate costume and each play the part of King Neptune's court. For instance, the ship's captain might play the part of King Neptune himself. What proceeds is a day of festivities, which builds camaraderie among the seafaring crew."

This tradition is so strong within the US Navy that your shellback status stays with you for the rest of your life. It's always been an honor for me being known as a US Navy shellback. Also, transiting the Panama Canal was a very rewarding experience for the entire crew.

Giving Back - Two

During our return trip home through the Panama Canal, each division requested volunteers to run laps around the ship's main deck. As a strong runner I volunteered to represent the Weapons Division. From the time we initially entered the canal to the point of exit, we had a sailor running laps. Each runner negotiated with other crew members on a paid fee per lap, usually twenty five cents per lap. Our goal was to raise money for the Red Cross. At the exit of the canal the crew had collectively ran enough laps to earn nine hundred sixty dollars for the Red Cross. Unknown to many civilians, it's common for the US Navy to provide good will services to ports of calls in need. Most good will services are performed "under the radar" and don't receive positive media attention. It was an honor for me when giving back to those in need, such as in Tela, Honduras.

Because we transited the Panama Canal and crossed the equatorial line, all crew members received large personalized (although unofficial) Navy certificates for both events. The certificate for crossing the equatorial line is entitled "Imperium Neptuni Regis" and the

146

certificate for transiting the Panama Canal is entitled "Order of the Ditch." Both certificates hang on a wall in my home office. Two incredible life experiences in one short cruise!

The Med Cruise

Upon returning from Nicaragua our ship was in homeport for about two weeks before preparations began for our extended duty overseas. Our Med Cruise was targeted to last eight months. As a newlywed I was not looking forward to spending many months away from my sweetheart. However, I was committed to serving honorably and performing my duties to the best of my abilities. At this point in my military career the slaughterhouse rules were instilled deep within me. I was accountable for ensuring the ship's gun and missile fire control system was combat ready. I had maintained and upheld my professional integrity to the UCMJ and the USS Gallery. I had built mutual respect with other sailors in my division and they entrusted me to operate and maintain the ship's weapon systems. Inclusive with supporting the slaughterhouse rules, I had earned and been advanced to the rank of Second Class Petty Officer (E5). Unknown to me, the USS Gallery's next duty station would test my resilience to its utmost.

Books

When I accepted the neutral duty in California my active duty time was cut from six to four years. Therefore, I did not receive the formal C School training that a six year enlistee would receive. The C School training would have taught me everything I needed to know about maintaining and operating the ship's gun and missile fire control system. Without formalized training, it was up to me to learn as much as

I could about operating, maintaining, testing and fixing the ship's weapon system. I spent many hours of my free time reading and studying the gun and missile fire control system technical manuals, schematics, maintenance program, operating instructions and testing documentation. I maintained a log book that I used to help me remember important processes and test points about the missile system. Spending significant amounts of time with my head in the documentation I earned the nickname "Books." I thoroughly enjoyed owning this new nickname. Thinking back, two years prior I had befriended the local hometown librarian so I could teach myself basic electronics and math principles to test into the Navy. Back then I was still working as a butcher workman in the slaughterhouse. A lot had changed in just over two years!

While in home port and preparing for our Med Cruise, each crew member was ordered to ensure our families were financially protected prior to shipping out. However, this time we knew we were heading for the Mediterranean Sea and, ultimately, the Persian Gulf. It was unknown specifically where the ship would be ported or any specifics of time, dates or defined routes. Our forward duty stations and ship's movement were only known to those sailors with the need to know. There is a saying in the Navy "Loose lips sink ships." Releasing information about the ship's movement is punishment as per the UCMJ. This type of information is considered confidential, if not secret. Our ship's departure date arrived and we said goodbye to our family and friends. We shipped out and headed east across the Atlantic on October 20, 1983.

Invasion of Grenada

During the second day of cruising east in the Atlantic, our ship met up with other Navy ships that came from Norfolk, Virginia, and Charleston, South Carolina. With approximately sixteen ships we formed an impressive armada of Navy military strength. Needless to say, I felt quite safe within the confines of the armada. On the third day of cruising east, one-third of the ships steered away from formation and headed to the small island of Grenada. I had never heard of Grenada and did not know why our Navy was headed towards the island. I quickly learned that President Ronald Reagan ordered the Marines to invade the island thereby ensuring the safety of approximately one thousand Americans from the island's Marxist regime. Our Navy brethren were ordered to Grenada for operational support and logistics.

Gibraltar and the Spanish Ship

The remaining ships in the armada made it to the west coast of Spain for re-fueling and replenishment of food stores. After a two day port of call, we headed southeast towards the Mediterranean Sea the "Med." The seas were calm and the sky was clear. Luckily for everyone on board, the crew experienced witnessing the Rock of Gibraltar. I was told by some of the ship's experienced sailors there was about a twenty percent chance to visually see this famous piece of land. Normally, obtaining a good visual was hindered by fog and inclement weather conditions. It turned out we were at the right place and at the right time.

While in the western Med our ship performed joint military exercises with a Spanish ship – the Langara. The Langara was a destroyer type of ship that mostly performed duty in and around the country of Spain. During an exercise with the Langara, I was nominated by my division's Senior Chief Petty Officer to be part of a sailor swap between ships. A total of eight sailors (three officers and five enlisted) from the Gallery were assigned to cross-deck over to the Langara. The personnel exchanges were beneficial to both navies and an opportunity to enhance the U.S. friendship with our Spanish counterparts. The assignment was purely political yet gave me an opportunity to experience military life aboard another country's Navy warship.

Those of us lucky enough to be picked for the transfer were immediately helicoptered between ships. I worked and lived on the Langara for four days. With very little Spanish language ability, I managed to assimilate myself with the crew while identifying and performing the expected diplomatic duties. Luckily for me, this included having two beers a day! Having a single beer during an evening meal was accepted in the Spanish Navy. Each day one of the Spanish petty officers would give me his daily beer ration. Hence, a two beer a day ration for us U.S. Navy sailors. As an assigned diplomat while on duty, I held myself to the Spanish military protocol. However, beyond the assigned duty there was time to get to know the Spanish sailors over a beer or two and watch a movie. The experience was memorable and I learned a lot about the Spanish Navy.

Lebanon Duty

During our cruise across the Atlantic Ocean, we learned that two suicide bombers driving separate trucks filled with explosives plowed into separate buildings housing U.S. Marines and French military forces inside Beirut, Lebanon. The suicide bombers killed two hundred forty one U.S. and fifty eight French military service members, plus another

150

six civilians. The Lebanese Civil War was in full motion. An obscure group entitled "Islamic Jihad" claimed responsibility. The intent of the Islamic Jihad terrorists was to get the Multinational Force – "MNF" out of Lebanon. Our ship was targeted for duty directly off the coast of Beirut, Lebanon as an integral supporting component to the MNF.

The duty station consisted of a small armada of US Naval ships positioned within visual distance of downtown Beirut. One of the ships stationed alongside the USS Gallery was the USS New Jersey. The New Jersey was a re-commissioned World War II battleship that was retrofitted with the latest military weaponry. As a guided missile frigate and escort vessel to the New Jersey, our ship's mission was to protect the New Jersey by engaging the enemy before the enemy could engage the New Jersey. Therefore, our ship was consistently positioned in the direct line of fire from any known or perceived enemy.

The USS Gallery was a ship designed with the concept of being minimally manned. Unfortunately for me and the crew, this meant there would be a "minimal loss" if the ship were to be destroyed and sink. Knowing we were labeled as expendable instilled a stronger and more persistent sense of duty within me. I was intensely focused during my watch station and willing to fight to the end. I calculated if it's them or me, I prefer it to be them. As a minimally manned ship, the maximum complement of two hundred six men meant taking on extra assignments outside your normal day-to-day work activities, plus extensive watch duty. For example, I was the division's education training officer, damage control officer and micro-miniature repair technician. Above and beyond the extra assignments, my main focus was becoming an integral component to operating and maintaining the ship's missile and gun fire control system.

While stationed directly off the coast of Beirut, our missile and gun radar systems had to be constantly ready and manned – twenty-four hours a day, seven days a week. The small complement of qualified Fire Control Technicians required our watch duty to be six hours on watch and six hours off watch. We called it port and starboard watch duty. Our watch duty consisted of sitting at the missile and gun control radar counsel watching and searching for any aggressive enemy targets. Six hours on, six hours off, six hours on, six hours off. In the off hours we were expected to maintain one hundred percent weapon system readiness (continuous maintenance), eat, sleep and bathe. Other Fire Control Technicians and I lived this routine for fifty two consecutive days. I averaged about five hours of sleep every two days and learned that I could sleep standing up or curled up on a cold steel deck. Due to the hostile environment and unknown abilities of the enemy, we were constantly under attack pressure. During those fifty two days we were in battle station mode multiple times. It was a very stressful time, and the crew deserved a break.

Liberty in Izmir

After the stressful Lebanon duty station, the crew was given one week of liberty in Izmir, Turkey. Izmir is the third most populated city in the country of Turkey and is located at the far western end of the country. It's an Aegean seacoast city with history dating back to ancient times. I was very fortunate to be allowed to take off for an entire week of liberty. I rented a hotel room at the Etap Hotel, while my wife flew over with other sailor's wives to share the week of liberty together. As a couple we experienced the nightlife of Izmir, shopping, restaurants and, most impressive of all, the gold market. The gold market was a city block of gold and jewelry shops lining both sides of a narrow street. At night the shops were well lighted making a walk down the street feel like you were walking into and through an oversized sparkling jewelry chest. It was an awesome experience. I purchased a fourteen karat gold necklace which I still wear off and on today. We also went on a full day trip to the ancient Greek ruins of the City of Ephesus. Nearby the City of Ephesus was the original placement for the House of the Virgin Mary. Today, the house location is a small one room chapel where tourists can visit and think in wonderment about the life of the Virgin Mary in and around Ephesus. On our return trip to Izmir we stopped off at a Turkish rug store. Beautiful handmade crafted Turkish rugs were available for sale and shipping back to the U.S. We passed on the rugs and spent our money on wearable jewelry.

The Persian Gulf

Our one week of liberty in Izmir ended and it was time to get back to serious military business. The next target for duty and patrol was The Persian Gulf ("the Gulf") with some operations in the Indian Ocean. To get to the Gulf, we began to transit the Suez Canal on February 1, 1984. This was our second major canal crossing inside one year. While transiting the Panama Canal we saw jungle to our right and jungle to our left. While transiting the Suez Canal you saw sand to your right and sand to your left. From a Suez Canal perspective, the view never seemed to change – just a whole lot of sand. The crew was awarded another large, personalized, unofficial Navy certificate for the Suez Canal transit. This certificate is entitled "Safari to Suez" and also resides on a wall in my home office.

With the Suez Canal behind us we cruised south through the Red Sea then stopped off in the key port country of Djibouti, Africa. Djibouti is strategically located near one of the world's busiest shipping lanes and situated at the Horn of Africa on the Gulf of Aden. This sea lane choke point is the controlling access point in and out of the Red Sea from the Arabian Sea and, eventually, the Indian Ocean. The country serves as a key refueling site for many ships, including U.S. Navy ships. An objective of the U.S. Navy is to ensure this choke point sea lane is kept open and accessible to all ocean going vessels – with the exception of pirates. In Djibouti we took on fuel, food and other stores in preparation for our Persian Gulf duty. While in port, I decided to walk outside the sea port area and take some pictures of the local town. Witnessing the extremely poor living conditions of local residents, I decided not to take pictures and immediately walked back to the ship.

After our re-fueling in Djibouti, we headed east and arrived in the Gulf through the Strait of Hormuz. The Strait of Hormuz is located between the Gulf of Oman and the Gulf and is the only passage in and out of the Gulf. It is one of the world's most strategically important sea lanes and another key choke point. Once again, our objective for serving in the Gulf was to ensure the sea lanes were kept open for all ocean going vessels – except pirates. The shipping lanes in the Gulf were so busy, on our radar screens it looked like a large, slow moving freeway of steel vessels. There were massive cargo and tanker vessels constantly cruising in a north/south direction. When leaving the Gulf, the ships were either full of crude oil, natural gas, or some other form of fossil based fuel. There were dozens of clustered oil platforms throughout the Gulf. On our radar screens they appeared to be small cities due to their geographic clustering. During the overnight hours their lights would illuminate the Gulf night appearing as though large complements of holiday lights adorned the Gulf waters.

Duty in the Persian Gulf was long and boring, yet sometimes eventful in unexpected ways. For example, the Forward Lookout was positioned at the forward most part of the ship – the bow. He was responsible for watching and identifying old partially submersed yet floating mines. These were mines left over from the Iran/Iraq war. Occasionally the forward lookout would spot something floating in the water and immediately report his findings to the bridge captain. On two occasions it was human bodies floating in the water. We assumed these were fisherman fishing out of small wooden fishing boats and got rammed by a crude oil tanker during the overnight. Luckily, we didn't come across any old floating semi-submersed mines. The sea lanes in the Gulf were busy and dangerous!

Our liberty for patrolling the Gulf sea lanes was in Manama, Bahrain. Manama is Bahrain's largest city and its capital. While on liberty the ship's crew would seek out local British pubs to help numb our senses. We also spent a few days of liberty in Al Jubayl, Saudi Arabia for some good will activities. Our tour of duty in the Gulf was coming to an end. It was now March 29, 1984, and we headed for a short port of call in Pakistan.

Prior to leaving the Mideast region, the ship stopped off for some liberty in Karachi, Pakistan on April 8, 1984. Karachi is located on the Arabian Sea coastline. As of 2013 its inhabitants totaled more than twenty three and one half million people. Karachi was a massively populated city even in 1984. Our liberty in Karachi was focused on shopping and purchasing items such as teakwood furniture and leather goods. Actually, anything handmade from teakwood was a sought after prize for many crew members. Spending time and money in Karachi was enjoyable; however, our focus was heading west and going home. Starting from the Gulf it takes thirty days to arrive at the east coast of the U.S. Along the planned sea route we would re-fuel on four separate occasions with a final re-fueling in Hamilton, Bermuda.

The ship arrived in our home port of Mayport on May 6, 1984. Along the docking pier an instrumental band played welcoming music, while many of my ship mates families and my wife eagerly waited to welcome us back onto U.S. soil. Everyone aboard was ecstatic to be back in the United States and in the arms of their families. Our tour of duty to the Eastern Mediterranean and the Gulf was complete.

While in home port our duty watch stations were every four days. Long gone were the port and starboard watches we endured off the coast of Beirut. Ever since the bombing attack on Pearl Harbor (December 7, 1941), the U.S. Navy is always ready to get underway and fight. Since that fateful day in Hawaii, there are always enough personnel aboard the ship and on active watch duty to respond in moment's notice to any outside enemy or threat. Our home port "down time" was scheduled for thirty days. After that thirty day period the ship was assigned new duties, mostly in and around the Caribbean Sea area. The majority of duty assignments were from two to three weeks in length - just long enough to be very thankful when pulling back into home port.

Punishments

In the real Navy, there are stiff repercussions for anyone taking part in illegal drugs, fighting, stealing or any violation related to the UCMJ. If a violation occurred while out to sea or in a foreign port, the punishment would not be delivered to the violator until the ship returned to home port. All violators would be summoned to a captain's mast just prior to entering home port. An example of violating the UCMJ that required a captain's mast was the use of illegal drugs. All ship board personnel were subjected to random urinalysis tests. You never knew when a test was going to be given nor did you know who would be tested. If you tested positive for an illegal drug the punishment was forty five, forty five, two fifty for two, and a stripe. This meant; forty five days restriction to the ship, forty five days of extra duty, a two hundred fifty dollar fine for two months, and a single reduction in rank with pay grade. Any second drug offence the violator was given the same punishment. However, if a violator was caught a third time, they were immediately kicked out of the Navy with a general discharge. I witnessed multiple people receiving this stiff punishment. I felt the punishment was justified given the criticality of everyone's job on the ship.

Another Fork in the Road

It was now early August, 1984 and my four year enlistment was coming to an end on September 24, 1984. There was not much time to make an important decision from the three tempting choices facing me:

1. Re-enlist in the Navy for another six years. This would guarantee me the opportunity to advance in rank to First Class Petty Officer – E6, plus a new advanced "C-School", duty station and a twenty one thousand dollar signing bonus.

2. Exit the Navy and accept one of the electronic technician jobs presented to me by various government contractors located on the east coast.

3. Exit the Navy and enroll in engineering school of an accredited college.

My wife and I discussed the options with purposeful intent. My ten year plan was still intact and I truly wanted to go to college and earn an engineering degree. However, the government contractors were offering very good money with outstanding benefits as a full time employee. The Navy had its cards on the table too. All options were viable and each of them held their own positives and negatives. I believed in long-term planning and knew in my heart that an engineering degree would provide greater long term value to my career and to my family. To me, it was short term pain for long term gain.

While assessing my future college options we had the opportunity to preview various schools and their programs. My wife's sister and her husband lived in Phoenix, Arizona. They were quite persuasive about us moving to Phoenix. So, we focused our attention on finding a college in the vicinity of my in-laws. One of the school prospects was DeVry Institute of Technology (DeVry). The DeVry recruiter did a wonderful job selling their engineering program to us. Plus, DeVry had a local school in the Phoenix area and close to the in-laws. Their program was designed over a three year term, worked on a trimester schedule and fit well within my ten year plan. Fortunately for me, I knew I wanted an engineering degree and eventually earn a living as an engineer. Everything seemed to fall into place and we picked DeVry Institute to earn my engineering degree. On September 24, 1984, we left the U.S. Navy to embark on a collegiate journey. Unbeknown to my wife and me, my college journey would have its own twists and turns.

Thoughts for You

If there was one key experience I took away from living and working on a Navy guided missile frigate, it would be teamwork. Everyone on board the USS Gallery knew their functional position and performed their duties to the best of their abilities. Each individual was dependent upon the person next to him to be successful. If one person failed at their assignment it could be a lethal proposition. Consistent training combined with dedicated maintenance helped to ensure all systems were up and running one hundred percent of the time. Each person was accountable for the success of his own job. Integrity was adhered to via the UCMJ. I witnessed resilience within myself and my shipmates during our fifty two consecutive days on port and starboard watches. Respect was earned by performing your job to the best of your ability. Trust was developed between ship mates when each person did what they said they would on a consistent basis. The slaughterhouse rules were in full force in the U.S. Navy and especially aboard the USS Gallery. For me and the ship's crew, failure was never an option!

Can you think of a situation when you experienced teamwork amongst co-workers, friends or family members? Did the team achieve its objectives? How did it make you feel? Or, do you yearn to become part of a team and experience an outcome created above and beyond any singular individual?

*****

"I can't change the direction of the wind, but I can adjust my sails to always reach my destination." Jimmy Dean

Chapter 11 - College Phase One

Transitional Curves

Leaving my shipmates behind was a difficult process. I had formed strong bonds with some of the other Fire Control Technicians in the Combat Systems Division. However, I had goals and objectives with lots of ambition to attain them. With goals and objectives comes change. My wife and I realized there were multiple transitions ahead of us. Migrating from military life to civilian life was not an easy transition. The strict protocol coupled with intense team work offered by the military quickly disappeared as a civilian. Then, entering college and becoming a full time student was another major transition. I had never been a full time college student and had more questions than answers. With focus toward building a better future, my wife and I quickly began packing and planning our move to Phoenix with a side trip to Northern Illinois. Knowing we would be on a tight budget during my time in college, we sold our second car (a 1972 Thunderbird). This placed my bicycle as my primary mode of transportation throughout the college years.

We had about two months before school started which gave us enough time to visit my daughter, family and friends in Northern Illinois. During our time at my home town it became readily apparent that my father desired to spend time with me. He invited me out for multiple rounds of golf, followed up with a beer together at a local pub. He asked me about life aboard ship and inquired about all my military experiences. The time we spent together was enjoyable, warming, and it

161

felt like the walls built between us were falling down. The feeling of mutual respect and a new friendship was showing promise.

While in Illinois, my wife and I began our preparations for the move to Phoenix. We loaded everything we could into our Toyota Celica and rented a small enclosed rental trailer. The trailer was filled with other personal belongings I had in storage while I served in the Navy. Our Illinois visit came to an end and we successfully made the journey to Phoenix. Temporarily staying with my in-laws, we searched and found a two bedroom apartment one mile from school and only three miles from the in-laws. The area was central to northwest Phoenix with a multitude of retail stores where I could find part-time work. I was paying child support on a monthly basis, therefore it was imperative that I obtained part-time retail work that fit into my monthly school schedule, plus covered the monthly payments.

I found work at a local Radio Shack store selling electronic components and equipment. The pay was set at minimum wage but was supplemented with monthly sales bonuses. The store manager was fixated on selling and beating monthly quotas which put extra stress on us sales associates to sell, sell, sell. I worked a minimum of twenty hours a week with most hours worked from Friday evenings to Sunday nights. By working more than twenty hours a week I qualified to receive outstanding health and insurance benefits. This significantly helped with our bottom line financials. Also, to help with financials coupled with an inner desire to serve, I joined the Active Navy Reserves for a two year enlistment. My wife found work at a local bank. So between our employments we effectively supported ourselves while I was a full-time engineering student at DeVry.

School Stresses and Grades

Transitioning from full-time military to full-time college student was a challenging and scary experience. Many of the students starting at DeVry came right out of high school or other technical schools in the area. They had taken Advanced Placement (AP) courses, were adept at studying, and already skilled in the field of mathematics. The education I received in the Navy was purely technical in nature and didn't focus on advanced mathematics or other curricula. Plus, I had no idea how to properly study or implement effective note taking.

During my first trimester at DeVry I took twenty-one credit hours while working between twenty and twenty-five hours a week at a stressful part-time sales job. I hired an algebra tutor to help with solving complex mathematical problems. My new tutor also helped me with effective note taking. I had a strong desire to learn and fully enjoyed the challenges of mathematics and the electronics engineering curriculum. However, the course work was very difficult for me and I had to work extra hard to keep up with the well prepared and younger students. At the end of my first trimester I posted straight A's! In all my years of prior public schooling I never earned a single "A" in any class. I was always an average student and had difficulty with math and science based courses. As a thirty year old college student I was applying myself to the best of my abilities and earning top grades in my class.

As the trimesters continued the course work became heavily math intensive. The engineering courses became more complex. I had to hire multiple tutors along the way to help me with physics and calculus. Besides difficult course work, some of the professors had very strong egos. They were difficult to learn from and seemed more self-centric than being effective teachers. Each student was required to figure out how to learn from each professor's individualism. That was not an easy proposition for an ex-slaughterhouse employee who recently stepped out of the Navy. I worked very hard with long hours studying and working the required labs. My grades were hovering around a "B" average which, from my perspective, was outstanding!

There were very few military veterans taking classes. The majority of students were between eighteen and twenty-five years of age. This made it difficult to link up with interested people to form study groups and together, solve complex engineering problems. With the exception of paid tutors, the majority of my collegiate work was performed alone. I am sure there were self-formed study groups, but I didn't know where they were nor was I invited into any particular group. I felt isolated and had to lean on tutors with the occasional professor or Teachers Assistant (TA) meeting for help. I was, however, maintaining a 3.0 grade point average.

When I was halfway into the DeVry program, a life impacting event changed the course of my planned three year college goal and threw a major curve ball into my ten year plan.

Family Tragedy

One evening while studying I received a phone call from my older sister. She told me our father had cancer and his prognosis didn't look good. Our father was dying from pancreatic cancer. He was only fifty three years old. The news was dreadful and sent shockwaves through the entire family.

For many years as a child, adolescent and young adult, my relationship with our father was poor at best. However, upon returning home from the Navy our relationship began to grow with greater collaboration and respect between father and son. Our father served in the US Airforce as a radio technician during the Korean War. With my Navy background and working my way through college we had found a new relationship. News of our father dying from an incurable cancer weighed heavily on my mind, heart and soul. I was between my sophomore and junior year of engineering school with many more very difficult classes looming on the horizon. Depending upon the coursework in a particular trimester, I was taking an average of fourteen to seventeen credit hours. I was also working twenty plus hours a week at a stressful part-time sales job. I began taking time off from my studies and the part-time job to fly to the Midwest to support and visit the family. My Radio Shack manager knew about my family situation and did everything he could to manage a flexible work schedule. The DeVry school administrators were not as supportive and expected me to uphold my existing class schedule within the current trimester. This meant that if I dropped a class, I would not receive any financial relief. When I found out about our father's incurable cancer, I was taking advanced physics and calculus courses with labs. I felt as though I had no choice but to do the best I could with my existing course work while managing a travel schedule and witnessing the slow and painful death of our father. Also, the airfare fees put unexpected debts on our credit card which placed undue financial stress on our marriage. I had a difficult time remembering content, maintaining focus and finding time to finish assignments. My grades during this time period dropped to mostly D's. I began losing weight and I contracted a bad case of eczema on the palms and fingers of both hands. The dry climate of Phoenix made the eczema worse. The stress placed upon me was absolutely unbearable. My life was stressed out to the maximum. Something definitely had to change or I was going to crash and burn.

Finally, at the end of the current trimester I walked into the DeVry administration office, quit all my classes and dropped out of college. I was required to have a brief exit interview with each of my professors. During an exit interview one of the professors sat in front of me and said I wasn't smart enough to be an engineer and I was doing the right thing to drop out. The professor did not have knowledge about the personal tragedy in my life but what he said was unacceptable. In pure anger and disbelief, I just laughed at him, said thank you and left the building - never to return. The stress of selling and making monthly sales quota at Radio Shack was not helping my personal situation. Shortly after dropping out of college, I put in my two week notice at Radio Shack.

Our father died on March 6, 1986. After the funeral my wife and I had to figure out what to do about my college situation. We discussed

166

various options. We talked about me finding a job – any job to help pay the bills. We also talked about other college options. I didn't want to give up on my college ambitions and dreams of becoming a successful engineer. However, I was unemployed and a college dropout with excessive credit card debt. The entire situation did not look good and the future was completely unknown. I wanted to transfer my applicable school credits to the local community college (Glendale Community College) and work my way into the university system (Arizona State University). It was not easy to convince my wife since I would most likely be in school for another three to four years. Even with the extended years of school ahead of us, we were still within the timeframe of my ten year plan schedule. My wife relented and we began planning for my second attempt at college.

Never, Never Give Up

I set up a meeting with one of the Glendale Community College's counselors to discuss transferring my academic credits over from DeVry Institute. I was happy to learn that Glendale Community College had an electronics engineering degree program that was tied directly to the state's university system. A student could attend Glendale Community College with a pre-planned curriculum that would transfer directly to Arizona State University. As soon as practical, I enrolled in Glendale Community College's electronics engineering program. If you took all applicable classes in this program you would graduate with an associate degree. However, I did not intend to take all the required classes and obtain an associate degree. Instead, at the right time, I would transfer all applicable credits over to Arizona State University's College of Engineering and Applied Sciences department. Once accepted at Arizona State I could focus my intentions on my goal of achieving a bachelor's degree.

To ensure I received full-time student classification, I signed up for taking at least twelve credit hours. While talking with the school administrator, I learned that as a full time student in an accredited college engineering program, the student was eligible to receive grants and other financial aid programs. For example, during my one year enrollment at the community college, I applied for and was awarded a $500 scholarship from a major electronics manufacturer. Any money earned or received as a paying your own way college student was very welcomed!

I found a part-time job at a local grocery store that had a small stereo and electronics department. My job was to manage the counter and help people purchase small electronic devices, rent videos and enjoy the retail experience. The pay was two and one-half times the base pay at Radio Shack but did not require the sales staff to sell based upon quotas. Hence, a part-time job that was easy to work, low stress and only one mile from our apartment. I made other life style changes too. I had been serving as an active Navy reservist for two years and had come to the end of my contract. During the two year contract I was required to travel to San Diego two weeks out of each year and perform military duties aboard a guided missile frigate. I was also required to perform duties one weekend each month at the local Navy reserve post in Phoenix. The reserve duty took time away from my study schedule, and impacted my weekend retail job that was needed to help pay the bills. I decided it was time to move one step further away from military duties. As per the Navy Reserves contract, I resigned my non-commissioned officer status, received my second honorable discharge and became a full-time civilian. Cutting the military umbilical cord allowed me to totally focus on my school studies and reduce personal stresses.

The community college was three miles west of our apartment and my part-time work was one mile north. My bicycle was still a primary and effective source of transportation. My grades at the community college jumped back up to a "B" average. Since my physics and calculus grades at DeVry were both D's, the classes did not transfer and I had to take them again. During the second semester at Glendale Community College I signed up to take calculus, chemistry and physics. Each class was rated as a four credit hour course. The calculus class met every day four times a week at 8:20 a.m. The physics and chemistry classes were three credit hours each with one credit hour of lab work with each class. Between classroom hours and the labs the credit hours for the semester totaled twelve hours, which is considered full-time student status. At the end of the semester I earned B's in all three classes. Given the difficulty and intensity of these classes, I vowed to never take calculus, chemistry and physics at the same time ever again!

My one year at Glendale Community College ended and I transferred all my applicable credits over to Arizona State University. There was only one small problem. The university campus was twenty-six miles southeast from our apartment. With the scholarship money and a small amount of savings, I purchased a car that would get me to/from school over the next two to three years. From that point forward I began commuting to/from the university via automobile and leveraging the local city bus route park and rides. It wasn't an easy commute. I drove five miles to a city bus stop. There was no place to park my car so I made an agreement with a local bar owner and was allowed to use his parking lot. From the bus stop it was a fifty minute bus ride to Arizona State University. I made this commute every day I had classes. The best part of the commute was the opportunity to read and study while sitting on the bus. The worst part of the commute was that it took three hours of total commute time each day.

Success & Graduation Day

I spent three years at Arizona State University. During my tenure I became the President of the Institute of Electrical & Electronics Engineers student chapter. I also maintained a B to B- grade point average. I still remember the day I finished my last pure math class – it felt like I had graduated! The professors at the university were demanding, but fair. If you applied yourself and worked diligently on your studies, the outcome was usually quite positive. I never missed a class and always sat in or near the front row. Sitting in a forward seat helped ensure I maintained engagement in the lesson. I enjoyed learning something new every day. The more I learned, the more I realized how much more there was to learn!

The engineering school at the university was popular enough to attract a number of military veterans. I had the wonderful pleasure of getting to know three other veterans that were enrolled in the program

170

and taking similar classes. We formed our own study group outside of classes and helped each other with solving difficult engineering problems. Instead of paying for tutors, I was an integral component to a great study group. All of us were married, had common education goals and were veterans. As such, we became good friends throughout our university school years. To this day I am still good friends with one of the veterans and his family.

During the final semester of my senior year, a list of companies sent their human resource representatives to interview selected student candidates for jobs. The competition for outstanding grades in all my engineering classes was intense and very real. My GPA was not the highest in the class nor was it competitive with other highly intelligent collegiate students. However, I brought to the table six years of military service (four years active duty and two years active reserve) and another eight years of real life problem solving experience. With this experience and a good GPA, I was one of the first students to be hired by a telecommunications company located in Denver, Colorado. So, prior to graduation, I was already lined up with my first paid engineering position.

On December 21, 1990, I graduated with my Bachelor of Science in Electronics Engineering Technology. The majority of my family attended the ceremony, including my thirteen year old daughter. Experiencing the graduation ceremony had a very positive impact on my daughter. I believe her experience watching her father graduate planted the seed of going to college deep within her. After the ceremony, our mother informed me *I was the first male in the history of our family to graduate college.* It was without a doubt one of the happiest and finest days of my life. Remember the ten year plan? I met my goals and accomplished my objective in ten years and six months.

Thoughts for You

The decision to leave the Navy and embark on a college career was a fork in the road that presented multiple choices and challenges. Again, I picked up the fork, put it in my pocket and moved forward to earning a college degree. As with many life experiences, I did not know nor did I expect to have a family tragedy while I was in the middle of my college career. My increased resilience coupled with my wife's support pulled me through the difficult moments in my college career. There were no short cuts, just a ton of hard work that required the use of all the slaughterhouse rules. My first attempt at college turned into a living nightmare. I remember thinking that if this is what college is about, I don't want anything to do with it. I had to dig deep within myself and find a way to attain my collegiate goals and find success within my ten year plan. In my mind the ten year plan looked like a straight line from year zero to year ten. In reality, there were many twists and turns along the path of success. I believe it's great to have a plan, but plans sometimes change. The key is to hold onto your dreams, goals and objectives. Doing so will turn your plan into a worthwhile journey. Along the journey I put trust in my family and truly respected my wife for hanging in there with me. My last three years of college turned out to be highly fulfilling and personally rewarding.

Nobody can take away the knowledge you have earned. Your knowledge can be from the street, school or a combination of the two environments. Think of this knowledge as your personal perpetual bank account of knowledge that is worth more than any material object. If I had to do it again, I would.

*****

"There are no short cuts to any place worth going." Beverly Sills

Chapter 12 - Business

Becoming the Engineer

Shortly after graduation my wife and I started planning for our move to Denver, Colorado. My position as a Network Systems Engineer was waiting for me at the downtown corporate office of US West Communications. This was a position in a large business environment that I had been working towards for many years. As a future member of the Network Engineering team, my starting annual pay was almost double what I had earned as a butcher workman in a slaughterhouse. Inclusive with the large increase in base pay, the healthcare and other financial benefits in my new position were much better than what was offered as a slaughterhouse laborer. Needless to say, the working conditions were incomparable to what I had experienced in the slaughterhouse. I was eager to start working at the corporate office and begin my career as a real-life engineer.

Throughout my college studies I took as many wireless systems engineering courses as possible. My targeted goal was to become a microwave systems engineer. I had years of experience working as a gun and missile radar technician aboard a Navy ship. This experience supported my college studies in wireless systems. However, my first duties within US West Communications were in the area of data networking. One of the on-boarding processes was to have an assigned seasoned engineer work in parallel with me until such time the team believed I could navigate the company's business processes while working with their many new advanced data technologies and services.

174

Through this tutelage, I learned the technical requirements of data networking (pre-World Wide Web) and became a valuable asset to the internal data networking team. The company was developing its first public offering of a data networking service and I was targeted as the lead engineer on the project. As the lead engineer I was required to comprehend the business metrics and marketing criteria of the service then transpose these requirements into a technical solution that could be sold in the marketplace. The final products from my desktop were the technical and user manuals supporting the new data service that was actively being sold to government and educational organizations.

Other internal engineering work efforts focused on developing and building out large optical networks inside and between metropolitan areas. I was fortunate enough to work with some outstanding network and optical engineers that tutored me on the vast amounts of information that consistently landed on my desktop. One of the engineers on the team had worked in the company for over thirty five years. He was one of the original engineers that developed the technical requirements for broadband data services to homes or businesses. The network team had incredible depth of knowledge and experience.

It seemed as though a new technology or technology based service was popping up on a monthly or quarterly basis. The speed of information management and the changes incurred inside the company kept the entire Networking Engineering team super busy. There was always more work to accomplish than qualified people to help solve problems. My first two years as an engineer were exciting and challenging.

Re-engineering the Engineers

During my second year of employment I learned that the company was going to initiate significant business process and managerial changes. The company's average employee age was getting older with approximately forty percent of them qualifying for retirement inside a ten year window. This meant the company had to make quick changes and start hiring younger people to fill management and non-management positions. Fortunately for me, I was placed on a fast-track leadership program for management that would encompass a full year of extracurricular leadership studies, meetings and conferences. I noticed many of the upper management team members were carrying around a book about Business Process Reengineering (BPR). The winds of change were on the horizon. There were new "buyouts" offered for employees with greater than thirty years of service. New internet-based digital services were being added to the host of services traditionally offered by the company. Many market-lagging and old traditional analog services were minimally supported or cut from the budget. Departments were being re-shaped with every business process scrutinized for effectiveness and efficiency.

I was placed into a BPR team with little or no experience in business process development or delivery. It was time to learn about business transformation, how departments operated on a process basis and the re-aligning of business processes for increasing efficiency and effectiveness. These corporate wide changes negatively affected employee morale. Many of the seasoned veterans in the business became dismayed with the new operational changes while the newly hired engineering managers eagerly accepted change and moved forward with building a digital information age future.

In the midst of all the change, I was offered a position with a new start-up department focused on defining the future of digital cellular systems and supporting services. These are today's digital wireless systems that support hand-held portable wireless devices such as phones, tablets and laptops. In 1992 the cellular based systems in use were primarily analogue in nature and owned by a single monopoly. The systems in 1992 could not support open wireless capability or any enhanced broadband digital services sold into the consumer marketplace. My position on this new team of wireless experts was in the area of architecture and network engineering. I was responsible for developing a network architecture that would support future digital service capabilities from cellular tower to cellular tower all across the United States. It was a position I readily enjoyed. A consistent supply of new learning curves, advanced technologies and team collaboration kept me fully engaged in the new and upcoming digital wireless marketplace.

College Phase Two

Living with constant change in both management and business processes seemed challenging for everyone in the company. There was the constant dark cloud of lay-offs that loomed over everyone's desktop. I had a strong desire to engage myself with advanced learning thereby increasing my value to the company. I wanted to increase my educational level above and beyond my B.S. degree in Electronics Engineering. I started researching local colleges that offered advanced degrees. At the time, the company was offering full tuition reimbursement providing the program was accepted by management and your grades were maintained at "B" or above. I decided not to pursue an M.S. in Engineering, with the fear this degree plan would label me as a technologist with little desire to work in management. After reviewing multiple Masters of Business Administration (MBA) programs I decided many of the offered programs were not right for me. After six months of outside research, I found an advanced degree program that truly excited me professionally and personally. The University of Denver (DU) offered a Masters of Technology Management at their local campus in Denver. Students in the program would meet once a week for four hours of evening classroom lecture, followed up with plenty of outside hours doing research, working in teams and writing papers. Unfortunately, there was a problem with my qualifications for acceptance into the program. As an engineer I did not possess any financial based courses that were required to qualify into the program. For acceptance into the program I had to take two prerequisite classes in business finance, earn a letter grade of "B" or better then re-apply. I accepted the challenge and over the next six months completed the required business finance course work with grades of "B" or better. I then re-applied into the program and was accepted.

I thoroughly enjoyed the one night per week lectures but had not anticipated the amount of individual work required each week outside the classroom. Many weeknights and most of every weekend were filled with course work studies that included research, writing papers and preparing defense strategies with everything written. The technology management program consisted of learning about technology strategy, business finance, marketing, and technology transfer. The program is known as an inter-disciplinary degree. This type of degree program suited my thirst for knowledge and expanded my thoughts about how to effectively and efficiently leverage new technologies into businesses.

Due to the long hours of outside classroom time, there was family sacrifice. Instead of doing the normal family evening or weekend activities, I was constantly being pulled into external project groups or the home office to work on my studies. Effective time management was required to support family needs, work activities and outside studies. I truly believed this type of degree program would provide value throughout my career path. With the six months of prerequisite courses added onto the existing program it took me four years to earn my M.S., Technology Management. It was a ton of work that took me on an educational journey and opened my mind to future possibilities. I guessed that if it were easy, everyone would have done it.

Moving On

I had been working with the company for five years. With the extensive process re-engineering and management changes happening, I found myself in search of a new career position outside of my current employer. There were many billions of dollars being invested in building out the country's broadband internet, including wireless systems. I placed my resume on an internet supported job board and started receiving phone calls and emails every day from recruiters all across the country. The demand for my background in optical, data, broadband and wireless systems engineering was extremely high! I interviewed with multiple companies and decided to accept a position with a start-up company located in the Kansas City, Kansas area. Of course, this would mean having to sell our house in Denver and move to Kansas City.

Change affects people in many different ways – positively and negatively. It seemed to negatively affect my wife more than me. I believe I process and manage change better than most people and accepted change as a learning experience with positive future possibilities. The Kansas based career position appeared very exciting to me and filled with great future possibilities. My wife was not excited about this move, nor was she excited about our previous move from Phoenix to Denver in early 1991. The continual change in my work environments, coupled with long hours of advanced degree studies and relocations put a strain on our relationship. To help manage the stresses and strains placed upon our relationship, we researched and hired a marriage counselor. We quickly learned that open communications was important to resolving our differences with relocating and career advancement.

I had not yet finished all my studies at DU. The only course work left to finish was my Capstone Project, otherwise known as an applied thesis. I talked with my academic counselor and we agreed I could work on my Capstone Project anywhere, anytime. There was, however, a one year time limit to finishing the project. Also, I had to travel back to Denver at least twice to meet with my counselor to ensure the project was in alignment with the college's academic rules and fit within the technology management framework. It was time to move onward to my second career position.

Building the Wireless Internet

The position offered in Kansas was with a start-up company entitled the Sprint Telecommunications Venture (STV). The STV was a partnership business venture between Sprint, Tele-Communications Inc., Comcast Corporation and Cox Communications. The STV was just being formed and was looking for people to help build a national wireless communications services network. Hired as a Network Systems Architect, I was partially responsible for developing their nationwide network systems architecture that supported next generation digital wireless services. Today, these wireless services are known as Personal Communications Service (PCS). When I started with STV the company was in the process of bidding at auction then purchasing a share of spectrum (wireless frequencies) from the Federal Communications Commission (FCC). These frequencies are needed to transmit future video, voice and data services over a cellular network that currently did not exist. The STV spent billions of dollars during the FCC's auctions to own spectrum share across most major markets in the United States.

Immediately following the success of the wireless frequency auctions, the STV changed its name to Sprint Spectrum. Somewhere in the middle of the business chaos, the company awarded major contracts to key equipment vendors to supply the technology that would ultimately become a national PCS network. The race was on for building out the first PCS nationwide network. The architecture team (consisting of four

181

of us) worked six and sometimes seven days a week throughout the first year of development. Expertise in the field of wireless systems engineering was sparse and in high demand. This meant wearing multiple hats and taking on higher level responsibilities. Specific business goals and objectives were targeted across multiple large metropolitan areas. Time was not on our side. The network had to be built and be in working order with "X" number of paying customers within two years. The hours were long and the work highly fulfilling. The two year deadline for acquiring new customers was constantly in my thoughts. The will, dedication, and resilience of the architecture team ensured that we achieved our goals and objectives placed upon us by the executive team.

In parallel with the long hours, I was expected to identify the title and subject matter of my Capstone Project, write up an outline, and submit it to my professor at DU for acceptance. I received acceptance of my Capstone Project proposal and in early 1996 started working on the required research. Detailed discussion of the applied thesis is beyond the intent of this book; however, for reference the title to the paper is "Integration of SS7 Message Traffic onto an Asynchronous Transfer Mode Architecture." I worked throughout 1996 on the paper and on December 3, 1996 the applied thesis was submitted to The University College, University of Denver for acceptance.

Prior to the end of 1996 the company changed its name to Sprint PCS. In December, 1996 I was awarded a congratulatory plaque that states; "For having both the will and faith you demonstrated in being an integral member of the Network Engineering and Operations Team that built the Sprint PCS Network". Also for this work effort, a Cell Site in Des Moines, Iowa entitled "DM03XC571" was named in my honor.

Having been recognized by the leadership team and my peers was a humbling, yet rewarding experience. Working with other like-minded people in conjunction with leading edge technologies was exciting and challenging. Knowing that I had put forth my best work effort that helped build the wireless Internet was very rewarding. But what was most important to me during my tenure at Sprint PCS was the knowledge and experience I gained with working inside a fast moving, well-funded, start-up venture.

Between the end of 1996 and mid-March, 1997 I made multiple trips to Denver to support and defend my applied thesis. Finally, I graduated on March 20, 1997 with the degree Masters of Technology Management.

Building the Packet Switched Internet

A key component to my work effort at Sprint PCS was focused on the broadband packet switching network that transported the video, voice, and data between cell sites and other network equipment facilities. With this knowledge and experience I was pursued for employment by one of the primary equipment vendors – Northern Telecom (Nortel). Nortel had a significant sales team presence in the Kansas City area. Sprint Corporation was one of their primary North American clients. Again, I was coming to a fork in the road and needed to make a decision whether to stay with Sprint PCS or jump over to Nortel's sales account team. I already knew the technology, had insight into the Sprint PCS nationwide network system and created relationships with mid to upper level management inside Sprint PCS. After some negotiations between companies I was given the green light to either accept the Systems Advisor position with Nortel or stay at Sprint PCS. A significant increase in base pay plus the opportunity to work with Nortel's leading edge packet switched technologies helped the decision process.

I accepted the position at Nortel and immediately began working on their sales account team as a Systems Advisor. The objective of the Systems Advisor position was to work with the direct sales people while supporting all technology and engineering requirements, thereby enabling the sales of products to the client. In this position, my direct client was Sprint PCS. My annual earnings were approximately ten times what I had earned working in the slaughterhouse, plus I truly loved my working environment and my role which was integral to a leading edge technology company.

Manufacturer vs. Service Provider

Working with Nortel, I learned about the business process of getting advanced technologies to market. Working with Sprint PCS I learned about the business process of implementing technology that enabled services to customers. Nortel was a manufacturer of telecommunications equipment and Sprint PCS was the service provider. These are two different types of companies with strong dependencies between each other. The service provider looks at the manufacturer to provide them with communications equipment that supports the current and future services targeted for market. The manufacturer enables the service provider's services by developing, manufacturing and shipping equipment aligned with services being sold to the service provider's customers. Service provider customers can be either residential, private/public business or government organizations. The knowledge I gained working on both sides of the business fence would be instrumental with future professional business decisions.

A Start-up in Silicon Valley

In the 1990's the telecommunications industry had become deregulated thereby creating many new start-up companies with significant new opportunities. Billions of dollars were being spent on leading edge technologies that enabled new services being transported around the internet. Money seemed to be everywhere with selling and buying of businesses popping up on a daily basis. My career had been riding the internet boom since the day I graduated from college. The first web browser had been sold into the consumer marketplace in 1993 and I was an early adopter of this technology. The speed of building out the World Wide Web (WWW) was literally at light speed. It seemed like everyone with a business plan written on the back of a napkin could make money. However, all good things usually change direction or come to an end.

While working with Nortel I learned that demand for our broadband packet switching systems was decreasing. Once the United States piece of the World Wide Web was built out, it was logical that the demand for our equipment into the Sprint PCS network slowed down to a small number of orders. Most of the new sales orders were based upon equipment upgrades to support new services. There was some succession planning to ensure older model equipment could be displaced with new technology, but these sales orders were many months into the future. I began to look around for a new career opportunity.

One of the new markets supported by the internet was Fixed Broadband Wireless services. These services would support broadband data networking using wireless technologies. Having a wireless background and a deep understanding of the internet, I was pursued by a start-up company out of San Jose, California. The company, Adaptive Broadband, was a leading integrator of high speed wireless data antennas and systems. The company was looking to expand their presence across the U.S., in multiple markets with product offerings. They needed people with a strong understanding of wireless systems and data networking experience. I was that person.

Still living in Kansas City, I left Nortel and began working for Adaptive Broadband as their Midwest Sales Director. One of my primary client targets was Sprint Corporation. Adaptive Broadband's technology fit well inside multiple divisions of Sprint Corporation. I was successful with positioning equipment for trials across three of Sprint's primary business units. Everything in the sales channels that I had developed was looking quite promising. I was now selling a leading edge wireless technology that had market demand, a very competitive price point and large enough customers to warrant the spending on technology trials.

In the late 1990's a new saying was created called the dot.com bubble, which was a historic speculative bubble that lasted from 1997–

2000. The word "speculative" is a key word. People were developing internet-based business plans that looked good on the outside but were supported by a highly volatile speculative market. By late 2000 the bubble had burst with speculative investment money ceasing to exist. Gone were the days of making money from a business plan written on the back of a napkin. In early 2001 the telecommunications market took a beating in the stock market. In 2001 it appeared as though more telecommunication companies were going out of business than staying in business. Adaptive Broadband was not an exception.

On July 26, 2001, Adaptive Broadband filed a Chapter 11 petition in the U.S. Bankruptcy Court for the North District of California. In parallel with this petition for bankruptcy, I found myself unemployed. Unfortunately, my employment history was solely within the telecommunications marketplace. Finding a new position in this field for the rest of 2001 would be a monumental task. Fortunately, I had earned enough money throughout the rise of open telecommunications and the buildout of the internet that I was financially secure. My wife and I were comfortable knowing that if either of us lost employment we could still pay the bills on a single salary.

Another fork in the road was upon me and it was time to make an important career decision. Find work with a company outside my core competency and the telecommunications industry or do my own thing. I decided it was a good time to start my own company.

Thoughts for You

Engrained in every decision point across the four companies I worked for between 1991 and 2001 were the slaughterhouse rules. Advancing my position within my career path was important to me. I had a strong desire to support my family and be the best engineer possible. I held myself accountable for all actions and decisions that led to what appeared as a wild and crazy career path.

Prior to becoming a college graduate, I assumed that working in the telecommunications industry would provide long term stable employment. My assumption was incorrect. The de-regulation of the industry had very fast, wide-sweeping effects on an industry rife with needed change. Being fresh out of college I did not fully grasp the magnitude of change the industry was about to embark upon. This is not an excuse but a work-in-process that I had to learn while advancing my career from one company to the next. Being accountable for my decisions was paramount to moving beyond the "now", yet realizing the future of my working career.

With change comes unwarranted stress that can be personally detrimental. It seemed as though change in the telecommunications industry had become the constant norm of the day. Due to the intense pressures in the industry, I witnessed people lose their personal and professional integrity. Integrity must be maintained to the best of your ability regardless of the circumstance. Do everything you can to hold your personal and professional integrity. Integrity is the cornerstone to an individual's ability to succeed in their personal and professional lives.

Mutual respect in the industry seemed to take a back seat to power and money at all cost. Again, treating others the way you would like to be treated is paramount to building strong and long lasting respectful relationships. I learned to have great respect for some people yet little respect for others. Why? Is it because the way I was treated or because people respond to increased stress in different ways or a combination of the two? Looking back on those ten years of gainful employment it's easy for me to remember those individuals whom garnered my greatest respect. I would work for those individuals again.

With each fork in the road came the opportunity to increase my resilience through learned responses. Accumulative experiences coupled with the right attitude can increase your level of resilience and change the shape of your life's future. I accept this statement as true and lived it multiple times. You can view your accumulative experiences as negative, positive or somewhat neutral. As you move through life and accumulate your experiences, you have the opportunity to collectively analyze these experiences as helpful and positive events that support your life today. Stated another way, resilience is knowledge learned from all collective life experiences.

I like to think of trust as the bank account that is always open. People want to be trusted by their work place relationships, family, and friends. Trust is always a welcoming deposit to the account. In the telecommunications industry throughout the 1990's, sometimes it was difficult to build trust in the workplace - mostly due to the constant change that engulfed the industry. People were rapidly coming and going from one new opportunity to the next. I found it necessary to build trust as quickly as possible. I worked at getting others' trust bank accounts as full as possible and as quickly as possible. I found that I could catch more flies with sugar than with salt and built many trusting relationships in the industry with some connections on-going today. The key take- away about trust is to honor your current trusted relationships because years down the road, you may find yourself valuing healthy relationships with those people whom you built trust with many years prior.

*****

"If you're offered a seat on a rocket ship, don't ask what seat! Just get on." Sheryl Sandberg

Chapter 13 - Entrepreneurship

Building Something from Nothing

Throughout my telecommunications career I often overheard people talk about doing their own thing, being their own boss, owning their own business. The idea of owning your own business sounded glamorous compared to working as an employee. This thought never made sense to me until I found myself in the middle of my fourth career transition, coupled with the collapse of my chosen industry. In July of 2001 I decided to strike out on my own and become my own boss.

Beyond Sweat Equity

Starting your own business is one thing; being successful at it is another. Regardless of the time, money and sweat equity you put into a business, a person may decide to obtain outside investors to help with capital and liquidity. There are outside financial resources available such as venture capital, angel investors, equity investors, your own money and money received from family and friends. There is a saying in business "It takes money to make money." With the right balance of investment a business can propel itself from good to great in a relatively short period of time.

It's vitally important to have the right mix of investment. Some outside investing firms may require a sitting board member on a newly formed Board of Directors. Other outside investment firms may require a percent equity stake in the business. Equity for money could easily be thirty percent or more ownership of the business. Family and friends might be happy with just getting their money back – including a small interest stipend and the personal satisfaction of watching you succeed. After learning about the true cost of investment money from outside investors, I decided to self-fund the business.

When I was a full-time employee inside a company I received healthcare benefits, access to 401K plans, financial bonuses, paid time off, and other bonuses for successful business programs. As an entrepreneur, I had to fend for myself. Healthcare plan costs are very expensive with high deductibles on individual plans. Until the business turns a profit, healthcare plans are usually paid from personal funds. You also have the option of investing a portion of your own net income from the business in other investment plans that are equivalent to 401K plans. This assumes the business would earn enough net income for the entrepreneur to afford taking a percentage for investment purposes. The bottom line is that when starting your own business and financing it yourself, you mange every penny as efficiently as possible.

You will work more hours on a new business than you ever worked in the corporate environment. However, as an entrepreneur the hours worked come with one hundred percent flexibility. Once the business begins to make a profit, you can start to pay yourself and, if lucky, take some vacation time. When people talk about starting their own business I like to tell them "If you're willing to jump into Lake Michigan, swimming the back stroke, with no life vest or support system, then go for it!" That's what it felt like at the start of my new business venture. There was a financial risk involved too. So, it's important you know your own risk tolerance. I had to personally accept my own level of risk and be willing to take risks above and beyond what a full-time paid employee position would offer. I realized I had to be willing to make mistakes, fail then try again, again, and again. Also, as a new entrepreneur I started thinking big about growing the business but acting small as an operator. Knowing I was confronting a start-up business on a defined budget, it was critical that I carefully managed business financials while investing money into growing the business operations. When I decided to start my own business, accept the financial risk, and plunge into the work I decided to give it one hundred ten percent of my best effort. The big questions were: what was I going to sell and how was I going to do it?

Pulled into risk management

I decided to sell myself as an interim Chief Technology Officer (CTO) to the small and mid-sized business market. I developed my first entrepreneurial based business card and called myself CTONow, short for Chief Technology Officer Now. From my own definition, the targeted client market consisted of businesses in any vertical industry with annual gross revenues from $5M to $500M.

Given the type of previous positions held, plus working specifically in the collapsed telecommunications industry, I had not built a professional network of contacts. Most of my working relationships were outside the local Kansas City market with the exception of Sprint Corporation. With the massive downturn in telecommunications, which included huge cuts in spending, Sprint Corporation was not on my target list of client prospects. Also, the company fell outside my targeted client size. I joined the local Chamber of Commerce and started networking my way through the business community. I found a couple of small opportunities as an interim CTO, but were short duration projects that paid the bills but nothing more.

During my time as an interim CTO, I kept getting pulled into business risk management issues. The majority of risk management issues focused on Information Technology (IT) systems and infrastructure. A light bulb went off in my head as I realized there was a demand for IT risk management consulting and advisory services. I spent time researching the targeted market and believed the entire small to mi-sized market was underserved in the risk management consulting and advisory area. I changed my business card from CTONow to ContingencyNow. The word contingency indicated that my consulting and advisory services were dedicated to helping companies develop, implement, and manage IT centric recovery plans. Living in the Kansas City area, I immediately connected myself with the Ewing Marion Kauffman Foundation in Kansas City, MO. This foundation supported entrepreneurs like me and other start-up companies. The first stop at the foundation was take a business marketing class that taught us how to develop brochures, slip sheets and content. Within three weeks I had developed some very powerful marketing content that would help me obtain new clients.

The IT Security Business

As a business owner and future IT security professional, one key piece of start-up business advice I learned from the Kauffman

Foundation was to build a business operating methodology that is reusable across multiple markets. Whatever you develop must be easily replicated over and over again, without having to re-invent the wheel. I learned this while I was building my company's operating methodology. Knowing I had the right formula for building a re-usable methodology, I immersed myself into developing the business processes and core templates that supported selling IT risk management projects. This might not sound like much fun, but it was work that I enjoyed because it was for my own company. I spent many nights burning the midnight oil, and developing content that would ultimately drive revenue into the business. I developed my own sales targets, marketing plan and marketing content. I also developed the reusable templates used for building IT systems' recovery plans for a wide variety of client prospects. This total work effort took approximately one full year to accomplish.

Throughout the first year of building the business, I kept networking in the local Kansas City market and getting to know my targeted client base. Once the templates were "good enough" and the reusable methodology was refined, it was time to acquire the first client. The first engagement consisted of working for free as a risk management consultant inside a professional colleague's business. We agreed that I would implement the IT systems recovery templates inside his business and all outcomes would be given to the business owner free of charge. The work took about three weeks to accomplish. However, we also agreed his business would become my first reference account, thereby helping me acquire future business.

I had the valuable opportunity to figure out what worked and what didn't work with the existing methodology and adjoining templates. Adjustments were made to the implementation methodology, thereby eliminating many of the up-front assumptions found to be incorrect. Also, I realized that each template required an in-depth user guide. I knew how the templates worked, but what if I wanted to hire a contractor to perform the work? I began writing user guides for each template. The user guides would be given to hired contractors on a per client engagement opportunity. Each contractor was required to follow the user guides, abide by the rules of engagement with each client and securely manage client data as directed in each guide. The strategy was that once a contractor was on-site with a client, I would become the program manager overseeing the work effort of each contractor. This would allow me to sell multiple projects to multiple client prospects, thereby increasing annual revenues. My goal was to hire someone that could replace me. This assumed the business growth was large enough to hire a full-time business technology executive to operate the business while I worked on obtaining bigger and better clients. Unfortunately, the business never grew large enough to where I could hire someone to replace me.

Success Through a Positive Mental Attitude

I quickly learned that growing the business was a very tough proposition. In the 2002 timeframe, I learned that most companies were not interested in spending money on IT operations risk management. I attempted to leverage the new Health Insurance Portability and Accountability Act (HIPAA) of 1996 to gain traction into the healthcare market. I spent about two years positioning my services into the healthcare industry. There were many Requests for Proposals (RFP's), emails, phone calls and, depending upon the location of the client prospect, a face-to-face meeting. One day I was on the phone talking with a hospital administrator of a County hospital. He abruptly told me that "When the HIPAA police show up at my doorstep, I will worry about it then." That was enough feedback for me to stop spending my time and energy on an industry that didn't want my services. However, I kept my positive mental attitude about my business. I knew my business services could provide great value to any small to mid-sized client.

I changed focus and began targeting financial institutions. Victory! I earned two new clients! One particular financial client kept my company on board for five years! Most work effort was based on short term projects helping a client fully understand its IT vulnerabilities, risks, strengths and then helping them develop a multi-year risk mitigation strategy. This included helping the client pull together a risk management budget that made sense to their business operations. The intent was to help each client effectively and efficiently invest in business operations risk management.

By 2006 the business was doing "OK", but not stellar. With weak revenues, I decided to develop a franchise model and began building a "Market Affiliate" (MA) program. The intent was to have a copy of me in every major metropolitan area market. Think of each major metropolitan market as the Tier one cities across the United States. All templates, supporting documentation, operation methodology, and framework would be supported from the main office. Each MA would keep a major percentage of it's revenues with the main office receiving a minor percentage. With ten, twenty, or thirty under management, the business would easily attain its ten year financial goal. I told myself that if annual revenues were not $10M or more by year ten, then I would exit the business.

In 2006 annual revenues were peaking around $500,000, a long way from the targeted $10M. Revenue from the business was very cyclic. I spent massive amounts of hours responding to RFP's with no revenue to show for it. If there were a strong client prospect, they were usually small with short-term projects. Besides these weak and cyclic revenues, my marriage suffered due to low income levels and excessive working hours. The business revenues were either flat or tapering in the wrong direction. I had a difficult time envisioning how the business was going to attain its ten year target unless something changed. Little did I know there were significant changes heading in my direction that presented multiple "forks in the road."

Thoughts for You

Despite the impact on my personal relationships and income, owning my own business had its rewards that are above and beyond any reward given to me as a full time employee working for a company. Yes, it takes money to keep the business doors open and pay the bills, but there were some key takeaways for me that I would like to share.

Making a Difference

Many people want to make a difference in their own lives, in the lives of others, or in their local communities. Starting a new business and growing it to great expectations gives people the opportunity to make a difference. I have met many entrepreneurs that have an inner desire to be successful. To these people, success could be measured on how much money is in their bank account or it could be something more intangible, such as making a social difference for themselves and others. Many highly successful business owners give their money and time to social causes they personally care about. This is a form of making a difference. Some business owners give money to help pay for a new library, museum, aquarium or new dug outs for a local Little League baseball league. Whatever the outlet is for giving back, the entrepreneur can be successful in many meaningful ways.

Serving Others

When you own a business and pay people to help you grow revenue, there is a feeling of self-fulfillment that can't be measured. Knowing that you are putting people to work and these people are working to support their families is a very honorable thing to do. In essence, you are in a position of serving others. Whether they are contractors or full time employees to the business, you have become responsible – to a degree, for their success. The business owner might start out as being the true leader whom everyone admires, respects and is willing to follow. As the business grows and morphs through its own success, the leader has an opportunity to become a servant leader to the enterprise and its clients. A person can own a financially growing business in a capitalist society, yet proactively serve others. You can tell when a servant leader is at the helm of a business – people will work there forever!

Gaining Knowledge

Deciding to strike out on your own as an independent entrepreneur takes courage. Prior to taking the plunge, I believe it's imperative that you should know yourself inside and out. Are you a risk averse or diverse person? Do you openly accept criticism and feedback? Are you willing to go the extra mile for a client or employee? And most importantly, can you maintain a positive mental attitude? I gained knowledge to the answers of these questions throughout the business building process. If you thirst for knowledge, then owning your own business is the right place to be.

Though my business did not become as successful as I had desired, I believe it was nonetheless a successful business. The business stood on its own, provided outstanding valuable services to clients, kept contractors working over multiple years, paid the family bills and always paid its fair share of taxes. If you have an inner desire to make a difference, serve others, or learn more than you have ever learned before, then "yes" you should start your own business.

*****

"When one door closes, another opens; but we often look so long and so regretfully upon the closed door that we do not see the one which has opened for us." Alexander Graham Bell.

Chapter 14 – Discovering New Potential

Starting in "The Business"

I have been often asked "How did you get into the entertainment business?" As strange as it might sound, on multiple occasions, people walked up and asked me if I wanted to get into the industry as a print model. I never ever thought about being a model, actor or doing anything related to the entertainment industry. I did not take theater in high school nor did I consider "the arts" while attending college. The only thing I knew about the entertainment business was what I learned from experiencing a motion picture via the screen in front of me.

During my time in regional sales for Adaptive Broadband, I would travel throughout the country to meet client prospects. On three separate occasions, while waiting between flights at various airports, I was approached by entertainment industry talent agents. They would ask me if I would consider being a print model. Knowing nothing of the modeling industry and believing the modeling industry was managed by less than stellar people, I shrugged off the advances, threw away their business cards, and went about my business. At the onset of building my risk management company, I attended various technology and business conferences throughout the Midwest. Conferences were great venues for networking, marketing and getting my business known. During the summer of 2001 I attended a local small business expo in Kansas City. While networking as an interim CTO, I was again approached by a talent agent. The agent was local to Kansas City and had a booth at the expo.

Since I was currently unemployed and had been approached on this very topic in the past, I thought I would check out what the agent had to offer. The local agent openly discussed with me how the modeling industry worked, expectations for getting work and how I could get started. I decided, what the heck, I might as well go for it and maybe make some money on the side while I was developing my risk management business. I signed a modeling contract with the local talent agency. Part of the agreement was that I would shave off my moustache and maintain myself in "model condition."

Within two weeks after signing the contract I booked my first print modeling job in an advertising and marketing campaign program for a new Maytag product. It was a one-day shoot in Des Moines, Iowa, and I was a father with a family in a home setting. At this first photo shoot I had absolutely no idea what to do or how to do it. I had never heard of a talent voucher and knew nothing about the process of getting paid. Fortunately for me, my "stage wife" had spent many years in the business and was very helpful with showing me what to do, how to do it and how to get paid. She was surprised to find out this was my first ever modeling job because I appeared to know what I was doing (not!). Was this the beginning of an entirely new journey in my life that was never expected, sought after, or desired? Would this new journey lead me to bigger and better jobs? Or was this type of work just a passing fad that would never amount to anything? At the time I had no answers to the questions. I did however, soon realize I could earn enough money to help pay the mortgage, plus the hours were flexible and coincided with my crazy work life as an entrepreneur.

Within the first month with the new talent agent, I had a "composite card" developed. A composite card is known as a comp card or zed card. This card shows various pictures of the model in different poses and environments. It also includes the model's physical characteristics and measurements. As an industry rule, it's absolutely imperative the model look like his/her card. The comp card is used as marketing tool for agents, managers and models. Think of it as the model's business card. Whenever there was an audition, I provided the production assistant my new card. Being a rookie in this industry required all marketing materials be paid by the model out of his or her own finances. I quickly learned the modeling industry was a business of its own and I had to manage my expenses and time as though I were operating a new business. Oh great, now I am pushing forward with starting two new businesses! Plus my wife thought I was half crazy, but the work did help pay the bills. This was a totally unexpected turn of events.

First Acting Class

My agent kept telling me I had a great commercial look and wanted me to think about taking acting classes to learn how to be effective in front of a camera. I had not thought about working in front of the camera and felt I was too busy with my startup company to mess around with taking acting classes. The agent persisted and referred me to a local acting coach – Andy Garrison of the Actor Training Studio (ATS) in Prairie Village, Kansas. From the ATS's website I read of an acting class opportunity to learn how to actively listen and effectively give presentations to audiences. This type of class was ideal for helping me connect with client prospects and give outstanding presentations. I called ATS, set up an appointment and the next thing I knew I was taking acting classes. Yes, acting classes did help me learn to actively listen to what people were saying, and to successfully present myself to audiences. Surprisingly, this was an immense help to me in my IT security and risk management business. Knowing how to actively listen and effectively present yourself as an executive is considered two highly desired skill sets. As an actor, if you do not truly hear another person's message, the conversation quickly turns into a one-way dialogue and becomes disjointed. It's the same outcome during high level business conversations. I took acting classes every week for one full year and really enjoyed the challenges. I decided to branch out and take additional classes from another coach in town. This coach specialized with training actors for performing in commercials.

My modeling agent was considered as a full service agency and started sending me out on commercial auditions. I was delighted to book a national commercial plus a plethora of local and regional spots. I also performed as a voice actor doing voice over work for two radio commercials. With the commercial work I qualified to join the American Federation of Television and Radio Artists – AFTRA. This was a key milestone for me to be certified as a professional actor, paid for my performances and paid for residuals with all future AFTRA based jobs. The work was challenging and required an artistic side of me that I didn't know existed. I enjoyed working with producers, directors and other artists while being creative in front of the camera.

Taking the Entertainer Plunge

Meanwhile, my IT security and risk management business was acquiring new clients, and the entertainment industry was demanding more of my acting and modeling skills. Working a full-time and part-time job consumed all my time and energy. But I was able to balance the workload of both jobs because I had a very flexible schedule. In the Fall of 2005 my business revenues were far below expectations and the entertainment business was a welcome supplement. I continued to be dedicated to growing my own business because I truly loved working it. Acquiring new clients and hiring people was difficult but very satisfying. However, I also wanted to be successful in the entertainment industry. Finding my newfound potential as a business owner/executive and entertainment industry professional was exciting and filled with promise.

Unknowingly I put quite a strain on my marriage and our relationship was quickly moving in the wrong direction. The on-going travel, splitting time between risk management executive and entertainer, placed unwanted stress with poor communication on the relationship with my wife. The stress and strain on the marriage was palpable. We sought help from a marriage counselor and did our best at building a bridge of communication. Despite these efforts to resolve our differences, I felt like we were moving farther apart as a couple. My wife wanted a solid foundation to live on, while I easily tolerated more risk in life and wanted to go in a new direction. I thought about either myself or both of us temporarily moving out to L.A., (the entertainment capital of the world). This would be a temporary arrangement and give us an opportunity to find out if I could be successful on the global stage in the entertainment industry. On multiple occasions I discussed the idea with my wife, but was refuted with each conversation. I didn't want to let go of my new found acting desires and wanted to find a way to make it a reality. I decided to develop a business plan thereby taking a very business approach to the idea of temporarily moving to L.A.

A Business Plan

In late 2005 I spent considerable time doing research about the entertainment industry in Southern California. The research included learning statistics of those actors that earn a living at acting, number of actors in my age group/category, known listed and targeted agents and managers, total cost of living in L.A. proper, and how long I believed it would take me to book my first job. I built a business case thinking I had enough information to sway my wife's position to my side of the fence. I presented the business case to my wife and daughter – who had already graduated college and was working full time. The feedback was "You want to do what?"; "You're crazy"; and "You shouldn't do it." Given the less than desirable feedback from my family, I shelved the idea and focused on immediate business needs. However, the dream of temporarily moving to L.A. and pursuing an acting career was still a very real desire within me.

The next six months I did more research about the acting industry in Southern California. Inclusive with learning more about the local L.A. acting environment, I was earning more commercial acting roles and print modeling jobs throughout the Midwest. I talked to my

Kansas City acting coach about my desire to move out to California. My coach was quite pro-active with the idea and when the time presented itself, offered to refer me to a couple of acting coaches currently working and living in the L.A. area. It became clear to me that if we were ever going to move out to L.A. and try to make it in the entertainment industry, it would most likely happen in the second half of 2006 or never happen at all.

By August of 2006 I was actively engaged as an actor in the Kansas City community. I had completely re-worked the original business plan for moving out to L.A. This time the plan included my strategy on how I was going to acquire new risk management clients through my consulting business. Again, I presented my desires and findings to the family. They realized I had become more serious about making the move and taking the risk. There was debate about financials and the viability of acquiring enough acting and IT security/risk management work to help pay all the bills. At the time I was project managing multiple clients through my risk management business. Plus, the business was web enabled making it easily portable. As a consultant and advisor in risk management, I could live just about anywhere and grow the business. In essence, I would be working both businesses (risk management and acting) in L.A., just as I was in Kansas City. My family could see that I had a strong desire to give my best effort in Hollywood. After some debate, my family agreed that I would temporarily move out to L.A. for a period of six months, but my wife would stay behind in Kansas City. I assumed this would give me enough time to acquire an agent and get some decent acting work. Besides, I was already a paid-in-full and qualified AFTRA actor, which positioned me as a stronger candidate to agents than a one-hundred percent non-union actor. On October 1st, 2006 I packed my 4x4 Ford pickup truck with everything I needed and started driving to L.A.

Thoughts for You

The potential to change or head into a new direction in a person's life is within each of us. All of us have the ability to discover new potential. When a new potential presents itself, many do not act upon the opportunity. Is this because of fear, uncertainty and doubt? For every new direction there is the balance between risk and reward. It's important to understand the type and magnitude of risks while maintaining a conservative approach to reward. To help mitigate the financial risks of temporarily moving out to L.A., I developed a business plan. As with most plans it was a work in progress that required many updates. I felt the greatest risk inherited with the business plan was financial. As a middle age adult I had to seriously think about the negative repercussions to our finances. L.A. is a very expensive place to live relative to the Midwest. All costs had to be considered in great detail. I calculated a very conservative revenue number and ensured I had back-up money for emergencies. Having a plan was great but the risks were still evident and real. I had to find an affordable place to live or risk being cash poor relatively quickly. If you find yourself moving your life in a different direction, be sure you understand the full extent of financial and personal costs and risks.

Do you dream of making change in your life? Do you believe you have the ability to discover new potential but are uncertain where or how to start? Acting on the potential may require all or some of the slaughterhouse rules. Maintaining personal integrity, being self-accountable, respecting yourself, showing resilience after a loss and putting trust in others will help you move your potential energy toward successful change.

*****

"Build your own dreams, or someone else will hire you to build theirs."
Farrah Gray

Chapter 15 - Hollywood

Getting Established in Los Angeles

The day before I left for L.A., I mailed an entire marketing packet to sixty talent agents throughout L.A., Ventura, Orange, and San Diego Counties. The marketing packet contained my headshot, resume, cover letter and business card. In Southern California you are legally allowed to have multiple agents as long as each agent resides in a different county. Southern California agents want their actors to live in the local area. If you are outside of the local area they will not pick you up as a new talent. So before I left Kansas, I acquired a newly assigned cell phone number with a local L.A. area code. I also had a temporary, but local, L.A. area address. This helped to show that I was a local resident. I was focused on signing with modeling and commercial agents as soon as possible.

On October 6th, 2006 I rolled into Southern California. My target was actually Oxnard, California, where I would live in a room of a house owned by my brother-in-law. This would be a very temporary two month living arrangement. The room was free but the driving distance to L.A. was forty-five miles one way. Each morning I would pull together a cooler filled with food that would suffice for the day. The traffic was very heavy so it was imperative that I was on the road prior to 6:30 a.m. I would commute into the city and live out of my truck for the entire day while calling on the targeted sixty talent agents. Within two weeks I had signed with two modeling agencies and a commercial agent. One modeling agent in L.A. and the other in San Diego. Both of the modeling agencies had received my marketing packet, called me on the phone and wanted me to come in for an audition.

The L.A. agency was one of the top agencies in Southern California, had an outstanding reputation and had been in the business for over forty years. When I showed up for my open call audition their waiting room was filled with young talented men and women in their twenties. I had just turned fifty and was the only person in the room wearing a sport coat with accompanying professional looking clothes. Everyone filled out the appropriate paperwork and waited their turn to meet with the head talent agent. After everyone auditioned we were sitting in the waiting room to hear either a "yes" or "no" answer. They would either sign you on the spot or they wouldn't. The head agent entered the waiting room, pointed to me and said "you stay", everyone else is a no. I received a few unwanted and disbelieving stares from the other models as they left the room. I immediately signed with this modeling agency.

Signing with my first commercial agent in L.A. was a completely different situation. I sent this commercial agent a marketing packet but never heard back from the agency. I decided to do a physical cold call by showing up at their front desk and ask to see their head commercial agent. When I showed up I was told the head agent was busy and unless I had an appointment I couldn't meet with him. I told the front desk clerk my story about sending in my marketing packet and I was certain if I could get a quick five minute meeting with the agent, he would sign me. Fortunately, the agent's office was adjacent to the front desk, his door was open, and he overheard the conversation. He came out, took a

211

quick look at me and invited me into his office. The commercial agent's office was located in a tall building on Melrose Avenue in mid-town L.A. Standing there in his expansive office with a North facing view, I could see the famous Hollywood sign up on the mountain. It was an incredible surreal moment for me. While standing there looking at the sign the agent pulled my marketing packet out from a small pile of other headshots – a very small pile! He began telling me I was in in the "short stack" and his assistant was going to call me to set up an appointment. As I was already in his office, he asked me about my acting plans and wanted to know more about me as a person. We were having good communication when I asked him about the very large stack of headshots resting on the edge of his desk. He immediately took a swiping forearm and pushed the entire pile into an oversized trash can next to his desk. He told me these were the "no's" and said he receives this number of submissions every day! After some more conversation he handed me his contract packet, told me to go home, read everything and if I was interested in signing with his agency, stop by with a signed contract. I suggested I could just sit in the lobby, read the content, and either sign it now or just leave. We agreed on the process. I read and I signed. Signing with a medium sized commercial agent was very fortunate! While living in L.A., I met actors that had been trying for two, three, or more years to sign with an agent without success.

During week two in the city, my commercial agent got me an audition at Paramount Studios for the upcoming feature film Charlie Wilson's War. It was for a very small role where I would play Julia Roberts' husband. Apparently my new commercial agent knew someone

212

of stature in the production team of the movie and got me an audition. I spent a half day on the Paramount Studios lot waiting my turn to audition for the role. After many hours of waiting, two production members came up to me and said that due to last minute script changes, they had decided not to hire anyone for the part. So, I didn't' get the job, but I did spend a wonderful half day in the middle of Paramount Studios. Not a bad start for a farm boy from the Midwest.

After commuting to/from L.A. via Oxnard for two months, I found a room to rent in Sherman Oaks, a suburb in the San Fernando Valley. I paid about the same amount for renting a room in Sherman Oaks as I paid for my entire house mortgage payment in Kansas City. Be advised, L.A. is a very expensive place to live compared to any city in the Midwest. Due to my in-depth analysis and business plan, I was prepared for the sticker shock. What I was not prepared for was the amount of driving time it took to get from point A to point B. When living in L.A. I had to constantly plan in advance my audition or business meeting routes the day before – and have a backup plan too. The traffic was very difficult and, if lucky, I could make three collective meetings (auditions and/or business meetings) in a single day. Over time, depending upon the time of day and where I had to go, I learned as many driving short cuts as possible. I became adept at driving the streets of L.A., and finding sufficient parking. The weather was a completely different situation. I must admit, the weather in Southern California was the best I had ever experienced. You never had to worry about the weather, only the traffic.

Endings and New Beginnings

I was four months into my six month temporary plan and realized there was absolutely no way I was going to achieve any of my acting goals within six months. Hollywood has a way of weeding out the short-timers and those who have a difficult time hearing "no" on a daily basis. I had no alternative plan for being a short-timer. I again attempted to talk my wife into selling the house and moving to L.A., but to no avail. Deep down, I didn't want to make the entertainment industry journey alone. However, my wife wasn't willing to move and I wasn't willing to give up on my dreams, goals and ambitions.

With deep sadness in my heart and restless nights, I decided it was time to end our marriage and go our separate ways. My level of risk taking and entrepreneurial adventures had taken its toll. It was too much to bear for my wife. Our relationship had been tenuous for many years. I held myself mostly accountable for the crumbling of the relationship. It was not an enjoyable time for either of us, but I believe we both knew it was the inevitable outcome. With a divorce looming in the short term, I began re-calculating my finances and putting together a new plan for living full-time, as a single man, in L.A.

A Key Property Purchase

Time has a way of moving forward with us or without us. Early in 2008, the housing crisis was in full swing in Southern California with tens of thousands of heavily distressed properties on the market. Many distressed properties were selling for less than fifty percent of their asking price of just two years prior. I decided it was time to start looking around to purchase property. I was tired of paying ridiculous amounts of money for renting a room and helping someone else pay off their home mortgage. After my divorce the vast majority of my money was invested in the stock market with a minimal cash position. To purchase a property in L.A., I knew I would have to sell the majority of my holdings in the market. I began putting together a financial plan that would support the purchase of a property ideally located in Sherman Oaks. This was prime real estate for me due to its location right next door to Hollywood, and a relatively decent commute to the majority of central L.A. locations. For the first half of 2008 I spent weekends driving in and out of targeted neighborhoods looking for a property that was within my planned budget. My financial plan was to have enough cash that I could afford a down payment between forty to fifty percent of the asking price. The market was heavily depressed so anyone with a big down payment in cash was in the driver's seat. It was a buyer's market with low interest rates.

With some planning and a bit of luck, in early August, 2008 I sold the vast majority of my stocks and moved the money (less taxes) into a cash fund. This was just six weeks before the stock market crashed! On September 16, 2008 the financial markets crashed and started the largest financial recession in United States history. This recession would have a positive effect on the future sale of my property, but a negative effect to my risk management business. With the majority of my money safely secured in cash, I had enough money for a hefty down payment on practically any property within my price range. In late August, 2008 I purchased a property in Sherman Oaks that was

215

selling forty eight percent below the asking price just eighteen months earlier. My new home was located five miles west of the famous Hollywood sign and three miles north of Mulholland Drive. The property was a four bedroom house with two full bathrooms, detached two-car garage, swimming pool, corner lot and only three blocks from a premier local school. Location, location!

The prior owners did not perform maintenance or invest money into basic upgrades, so the property needed some work. As an ex-farm hand I could repair just about anything. My new home was a perfect fit for me and my multitude of hands-on skills. Before moving into the property I spent a couple of months painting, performing repairs, and other basic upgrades. Once I felt the property was move-in ready, I moved into my new home. After getting myself settled I started the process of soliciting two full sized bedrooms with a shared bathroom to rent. I advertised on Craigslist and began the interview process. I was looking for single males or females who were gainfully employed, financially secure, and had some type of short or long term career plan. I eventually rented two rooms of the house to single men for an amount that paid for the monthly mortgage. With my living situation secured and my financials in excellent condition, it was time to focus on increasing the number of risk management clients and finding paid acting jobs.

The Business of Acting

The facts are daunting. The chances of being a successful start-up business owner are seriously stacked against you. The chances of "making it" as an actor (male or female) in the entertainment industry are much worse. The remainder of this chapter will discuss my acting life experiences and the entertainment industry knowledge I gained while fully engaging myself in the L.A. acting community. My primary focus was pursuing the film and television industries from a model/actor perspective. Hold on, it's going to be an interesting ride!

A Different Kind of Show

In Hollywood, there is no such thing as "show acting." It's called "show business" for a reason. People are in the entertainment industry because they love the work and have a strong desire to earn a living either in front or behind the camera. As an actor, my first job was to understand that I am the product and that people would hire me to help them solve a problem. That problem is to find an actor that can best articulate the emotional, physical and verbal responses of a defined character as written by the writer. If I was identified as one of the well suited actors for a specific role, I had a very good chance of being hired. I would be hired through the audition process which is managed by casting agents and/or their subordinates. Casting agents are hired by production companies to go out and find (in their subjective process) the most qualified actor(s). So, before I ever heard about a particular audition, the process of show business has been rolling along for weeks and sometimes months. Production companies have already acquired the needed money to invest in their project. The project could be an industrial film, full length feature or short film. Or, the project could be a made for television movie, television situation comedy (sitcom), or a web-based series. Production companies invest a percentage of the total

217

project development costs into their own projects. There are other investors that participate in the financials too. When executive producers are listed in the credits, these individuals are usually the primary or third party investors who have invested money into the project.

With many millions of dollars at stake, it becomes imperative to find the highest skilled actors to fill all open positions, thereby decreasing the perceived level of risk per investor. The investment risk resides on the ability of the casting company to find the best fit actors. If casting doesn't produce the talent expected by the production company, their reputation could be negatively scrutinized, thereby losing future business from the production company. So, actors are an important piece to the whole production process. As the number of scenes the actor appears in increases, so does the importance of the role to the entire script. Hence, popular lead actors can either make or break a project. Here is an example:

Let's say you are a star A-list actor and the production company wants to put you under contract to earn a maximum of $5M to work a project. The lay person who does not know the business of show business might think that $5M is an excessive amount of money for any single actor to earn on one project. However, as an A-list actor known to draw a large viewing audience, the production company looks at the $5M as an investment to the success of the project. If the project grosses $100M worldwide over a two year time frame, the $5M paid to their star A-list actor is money well spent!

Actor as a Product

While I was busy finding my way around Hollywood and going to auditions, I learned that I had to market myself as the product being sold to the Hollywood studios, producers and directors. In Hollywood, work begets work and I had full intention of getting as much work as possible. I believed that consistent marketing helped with getting my name recognized above the other tens of thousands of actors in L.A. There were many thousands of actors vying for a small pool of "good paying" acting jobs. With the sheer number of people, it was easy to find myself out of sight and out of the minds of producers and directors. My intention for marketing was to keep my name at the top of the mind of as many decision makers as possible.

I believed people would hire me for acting jobs because of my acting ability, appearance, appeal, perceived trustworthiness, and the ability to park my ego at the door. People in Hollywood like to hire people that are nice, professional, and able to proactively communicate with others while auditioning or on the production set. With a limited budget I pulled together a marketing campaign. I built myself an on-line presence through the Internet Movie Database (IMDB) and started my own professional acting web site. I had hundreds of full color four inch by six inch marketing cards developed. Each card included my latest headshot photo in reduced size. I researched and made lists of production companies, casting directors, agents, and managers. After every booking, regardless of how small the role, I would physically mail a marketing card to as many Hollywood contacts as possible to inform them I had booked a job. I had actor-centric business cards developed that I gave to individuals when networking at parties, screenings and other Hollywood functions. My business card contained a picture of my recent headshot, email address, cell phone, and the address to my acting web site. I always ensured I looked like my headshot, kept myself well-groomed, and stayed in athletic physical shape.

Sometimes at auditions, the casting director would say, "Haven't I seen you before?" or "You look familiar." When I heard those words I knew my marketing efforts were working. So, in the world of Hollywood I thought of myself as a contractor for hire, and then identified everything I needed to market myself as a show business contractor.

This process was very similar to starting a business. Putting together a marketing strategy helped to ensure the right people at the right time knew about my business and its value. Selling business value to key decision makers increases revenue opportunities. Propelling a new business forward requires a team approach, and that applied equally well to the acting business. Unfortunately, most actors don't realize the need to build a team that can help propel their career forward. They don't learn about the business of acting during their theatrical college days. When they move to L.A. the learning process of show business hits them full force. The actor must figure out how to be a multi-faceted business performer. The actor needs a marketing plan, training budget for acting coaches, a manager, an agent, and legal representation. The team approach is very business oriented, but required if the actor is serious about their career. I met countless actors with minimal or no representation and had no idea how to build a trusted team. These actors were prime targets for scam artists or anyone selling them self as a manager or agent with only a business card. With tens of thousands of actors living in Southern California, there were plenty of opportunities for the less than scrupulous to steal their dreams and take their money.

The A, B, and C List

The A-List

Have you heard people talk about the "A" list of actors in Hollywood? There are actually three lists; A, B, and C. The A-list actors are those individuals that are being paid the most and have received the greatest amount of air and face time. They are the big time players that have star representation. The A-listers have their own publicists, managers, agents, and lawyers. Good publicists representing A-list actors submit their clients into magazines and other media so their image remains in the minds of subscribers. It's all about selective marketing and getting the most bang for the buck. Sometimes their support team is made up of people inside a single large A-list agency such as Creative Artists Agency (CAA). Other actors pull together a virtual team from various sources. To be represented by an A-list agency you have to show considerable credits (working experience). Many actors get referred into an A-list agency by a well-known agent, manager, another A-list actor, or by being known to someone through a family or friend connection. As an unknown actor in Hollywood, the last thing I wanted was to be represented by an A-list agency. This might appear to be counterintuitive. However, these agencies are very busy with an extensive list of top tier clients. As an unknown actor in Hollywood, I targeted B-list agencies to represent me because I lacked outstanding referrals. Plus, I would have been buried at the bottom of their A-list names and never receive any face time with my representative.

The B-List

The B-list agencies are numerous and mostly tend towards actors such as myself. They target actors with good credits, who are qualified to join one or more unions and have a consistent training record. The B-list agents, representatives, and third parties are hungry to be successful and climb the Hollywood ladder. They tend to look for those actors that are hungry too. As a B-list actor I was continually on the lookout for solid representation by a B-list theatrical (film and television) agency. I had already signed with a B-list commercial agent but did not get signed by a theatrical agent. Theatrical agents are quite selective who they sign and require a full interview just to be considered. Interviewing consists of sitting down with one of the agency's directors, talking about your career path, helping him or her get to know you as a person, and performing a monologue, cold read, or both. As with the A-list agencies, it was best to get a personal referral into their office. It's the same with networking and finding a corporate job. You get placed in the short stack of resumes with a solid, personal referral.

The C-List

As an unknown actor, it's easy to find yourself working long hours for free or earning very little money. Plus, there is greater opportunity of being used and abused by unscrupulous producers and directors. Without managerial or agency representation, actors are powerless to negotiate terms and conditions of an agreement. In

222

Southern California, there are significant amounts of non-union acting jobs that pay very little or nothing at all. From student films, to projects that have deferred payment schemes, they usually pay nothing or one hundred dollars a day (or less). This is where the C-List agencies and anyone with a business card reside. Actors may find themselves sitting around an entire day or night waiting to be placed into a project all the while eating crappy food and, if lucky, receiving enough water to stay hydrated.

When I lived in Kansas City, I worked for free on many small acting projects. My objective was to build an acting resume –which I did. The Hollywood scene was very much the same. I had to build out a resume before anyone from the B or A-list would look at me. However, there comes a time when working for free or for less than one hundred dollars per day is unacceptable. There were occasions when people asked me to be in their project, work a table read, or help on a set, and I said "Thanks, but no thanks." I didn't see the value of redundant work that paid nothing and added another unimpressive credit to my resume. Taking on too much C-level work can be perceived as being cheap, inexperienced, and an easy target for being offered low wages.

There are people in the entertainment industry that market themselves as capable of getting you paid acting jobs. For the most part, these people deliver very little or nothing. The majority of this advertised work is for free or pays very little and provides minimal value for a professional actor. In the corporate business world they are called "empty suits." The C-list agencies, their people and third party companies that represent them are in a world of their own. From my perspective, these are the bottom feeders of the entertainment industry. They are less scrupulous and willing to say just about anything to get the actor to part with their talent, time and money. Fortunately for the bottom feeders there was a never-ending supply of actors moving into L.A. It's like a large revolving door of never-ending talent in search of making it big in the industry. The new talent bring with them dreams and ambitions of stardom and a perceived luxurious new way of life. For these tens of thousands of dream chasers, the C-list people pray on the actor's hopes, take their money and leave them empty inside and out. In essence, they steal the soul of the unwitting actors' dreams.

I was already of middle age and had plenty of business, military, and overall street smart knowledge. I could readily tell if someone had the capability of paying me for acting work. If they talked a great story but didn't produce a valid contract that was represented by SAG or AFTRA, then I would either negotiate a better role with increased pay or say "No, thank you." The "C-listers" (that is what I call them) did not encompass a high degree of integrity or trust. From a slaughterhouse rules perspective, they didn't pass the test. When working with the C-list people, if it sounded too good to be true, then most likely it was.

Getting Into SAG-AFTRA

I earned my Screen Actors Guild (SAG) card in January, 2011. Earning that card was a very long, arduous and frustrating task. It took me five years. But first, a little bit of history. When I was performing as an AFTRA actor the two unions – SAG and AFTRA, were completely separate. You had to earn your way into each organization on your own merit with differing requirements. Since January 2011, SAG and AFTRA have joined forces and created one single entity called SAG-AFTRA. Prior to the merger an actor could "qualify" to enter SAG by acquiring three SAG vouchers. A voucher was earned by a non-union actor when the actor performed on a SAG production either in a principle role or as a background performer. Sounds easy enough but there's a catch. SAG productions are required to fill their background spots with SAG background actors first. However, let's say that at the time of production a SAG background actor (or two, or three) did not show up for work. The production team had the ability to hire a non-union background performer. The voucher earned for that day's work was marked as a SAG production voucher and the non-union actor earned one voucher. The trick was to get submitted into SAG projects and earn three vouchers. This process may take a week, month or years. The time was quite dependent upon the actor's ability to have built a supporting team that had the actor's best interest in mind. Or, the non-union actor could be asked to join a SAG production through friends and family (Hollywood is well known for its nepotism). If the non-union actor was lucky to be awarded a principle role with speaking lines, this automatically qualified the actor to join SAG (don't hold your breath on getting this opportunity). In either situation the actor was eligible to join SAG but was not yet in SAG. Many actors are considered SAGe, which means SAG eligible. The second catch was the buy-in fee. In January 2011, the buy-in fee was two thousand three hundred dollars. That might not appear to be a very large sum of money. However, as a non-union actor working at less than one-hundred dollars per day, twenty-three

225

hundred was a big number! It can be quite difficult getting placed on a SAG production set, which is why is requires a team approach. Those actors who had an agent /or manager making phone calls and sending emails on their behalf had a greater success rate.

I had earned two SAG vouchers over a period of three years. It took me two more years to earn one more voucher. I ended up being hired by "SAG" friends that were developing a web series called Game Night. They were looking for a guy who could pass as a Harley Davidson biker type but with a fun demeanor. I was hired to play a principle role in the series. This earned me my third and final SAG voucher. I filled out the required documentation, wrote a check for two thousand three hundred dollars, then drove to the SAG office located on Wilshire Blvd., and submitted my hard earned qualifications. Immediately after joining SAG, I began looking for a theatrical agent and a manager. Within two months I had signed with a theatrical agent and a new manager. Being a SAG card carrying member made a huge difference! Also, I had some really great credits on my resume.

Peaks and Valleys

Regardless of where anyone is in their career, there will be peaks and valleys along the continuum of success. I found myself working extremely hard at ensuring every acting audition was perceived from the auditor as an outstanding audition. I held myself accountable for showing up on time. I did the best I could to ensure there was enough spare time in the waiting room to mentally prepare for the audition. I respected other actors' space by keeping to myself and not engaging in useless talk while waiting my turn. Once in the audition room I did the best I could with fulfilling the writer's vision of the character, and I put my heart and soul into every character with every audition.

On many occasions I would receive a character role from my agent or manager that appeared as though it was written just for me. When these roles presented themselves, my psyche was filled with all the wonderful outcomes and possibilities. After the audition I felt like I did extremely well and believed that I would make it to the short list of actors who would receive a call back. Once called back, I had the opportunity to audition and meet with the producer, director, writer, or any combination of the production team. To receive a call back was very exciting! When I received a call back, I felt like I had some level of control over the outcome of the decision process. It was make or break time and I was always determined to make it. This was the peak of the audition process. I had the right character, an awesome script, a call back and the training needed to succeed. What a wonderful feeling!

After a call back audition I might hear nothing from my manager and/or agent. I would wait days before I started calling and asking if they had heard back from production. Did I pass the final audition? Did I bomb? Did the production team lose their funding? What was the final outcome of all the work effort put forth into the audition process? Sometimes I would receive a call telling me the outcome went in a different direction, that I didn't get the part. This was the mental and emotional low end of the valley for an actor. I would feel as though all the air was let out of my acting tires. Additionally, I would not receive any feedback as to why I didn't get the part. This was a difficult situation for anyone to experience. Being resilient, holding yourself accountable, and trusting the acting process was extremely important to surviving the low valleys.

As a working actor, I experienced the peaks and valleys of the process many times. For the consummate actor, it's a way of life. The problem is that this roller coaster of emotions can continue for years. To help me manage the stresses and strains of my peaks and valleys, I would work exclusively on my risk management consulting business. This would help re-set my mental attitude and breathe new life in my desire to acquire acting roles. When I would begin to think negatively about the acting profession in Hollywood, I knew it was time to take a short break. Taking short breaks throughout the years in Hollywood helped me keep a positive perspective on my goals and objectives. I knew that Hollywood wasn't going away and there would always be another new film or television program on the horizon. My consulting business had earned new clients that kept my risk management knowledge and experience front and center. The flexibility of my work schedule enabled success in both acting and risk management consulting.

Meeting Great People

When I wasn't rushing off to an audition or at a client site as a risk management professional, I was actively networking and getting involved in outside organizations or other Hollywood events. My intention was to network with as many A-List actors and other industry professionals as possible. For example, I attended events hosted by Women in Film. I signed up to preview and give feedback on upcoming

228

motion pictures, attended art gallery open houses and volunteered to help with casting on other major projects. I also got myself booked on various shows as a featured extra, which put me front and center working with A-List actors on premier film sets and television shows. Along the way I met some really great people. Here is a short list of some of those people:

Dustin Hoffman. I had the wonderful pleasure of sipping some fine wine alongside Dustin while attending a Women in Film event, where he was the keynote speaker. I showed up early and found Dustin standing alone at the bar holding a glass of wine. I approached him, introduced myself and asked him what he did for a living? He answered "I am still trying to figure that out." After a quick laugh between us I extended the conversation and learned about his fascinating acting journey. I quickly learned Dustin is a truly wonderful person and a highly professional actor.

Peter Fonda. While attending a pre-screening for the motion picture "3:10 to Yuma", I met Peter after the screening. He was on stage doing a Q&A session. Immediately after the session I approached him and started talking about horses and Harley Davidson motorcycles. In 1969 Peter Fonda had a primary role in a movie entitled "Easy Rider", where he, Dennis Hopper and Jack Nicholson rode across the country on Harley Davidson motorcycles. The film has since become a cult classic. We had a great conversation talking about our commonalities with motorcycles and horses.

Simon Cowell. I met Simon during an art gallery open house on Rodeo Drive, in Beverly Hills. Once Simon entered the gallery I approached him and started talking about cars. A specialty auto dealer was standing alongside listening to our conversation and offered Simon to check out his newest and latest sports car parked on Rodeo Drive. After a few minutes of maneuvering through the people, I found myself sitting in a very expensive sports car, drinking wine, and having a great conversation about sports cars with Simon.

Louis Gossett Jr. I met Louis and his wife at a breakfast networking event in Malibu. Louis was the guest speaker and talked passionately about his non-profit foundation entitled "Eracism Foundation." I found Louis to be an inspiring and wonderful person, focused on helping others and a great actor.

Ashton Kutcher. I met Ashton while working on the feature film set of "Spread." Ashton was very professional and easy to work with during the long hot days of filming at a local Beverly Hills pool. I learned that Ashton was a busy man in Hollywood, took his acting work very seriously and brought to the table a positive and professional attitude about show business.

Holland Taylor. I was very lucky to land a front and center role on the set of "Two and a Half Men." While on set, I was placed on the front room sofa with Holland. Talking with her off and on during the full day shoot was positively enlightening. Holland is very professional and I have great respect for her acting skills and long standing acting career that stretched from New York theatre to Hollywood.

Life-Work Balance

As a full time actor living in L.A., the road to success is a very long and arduous path for most people. There are individuals who move into the city and within their first two years hit it big and become the next upwardly mobile movie star. The chance of hitting it big early in your acting career is very small – don't hold your breath.

Perceiving years of work ahead and an endless supply of rejection, it's important to maintain a work-life balance. The actor must have some form of other income to help pay the bills while he or she is taking acting classes and going to auditions. My primary income came from my risk management consulting business. If I was at a client site I would "book out" from my agents and manager. This meant I wasn't available for auditions. It's customary and required by managers and agents to have their actor's book out when not available.

Most, if not all, auditions are set during the working hours of each day. This leaves the evenings and nights open for the actor to find work that, hopefully, pays the bills. Because of the scheduling, one of the most difficult jobs to get in L.A. is bartending. It appeared to me that every bar had a wait list of actors desiring to be hired as a bartender. Back at my home town in Illinois a bartending job was not hot on the job list for anyone. In L.A., it's the exact opposite!

Working as an IT security and risk management consultant, I would find companies that had a strong interest in contracting me as their business security advisor. As a contractor, my schedule was flexible thereby allowing me to audition for acting jobs while working client projects. I met other actors who were also contracting engineers, mathematicians, chemists, handymen, or business entrepreneurs searching for their next infusion of money for a start-up business. Those actors whom struggled to find jobs that paid enough to cover all their bills had short lived acting careers in L.A. Bartending and waiting tables was the norm for the acting community. Unfortunately, the better paying service jobs had long wait lists of actors desiring to be hired. I was very fortunate because my risk management business paid the bills while any money earned as an actor and model was saved in an emergency fund. I owned my own property, had renters that paid the mortgage, and was growing equity for future value. I was quite happy with my work-life balance, housing and financial situation.

Finding New Love

After I moved to L.A. and post my divorce, the very last thing I wanted in my life was to develop another relationship or to become part of the dating scene. I felt as though I needed time to myself. I used my free time to analyze and learn what went wrong with my previous relationship. Also, to heal the emotional wounds that resided deep within me. I had a strong desire to re-focus my time and energy on growing my risk management business, while finding work as an actor and model. I spent the majority of free time reading or, on occasion, checking out one of the local beaches.

A year had passed and I felt ready to start looking for a new relationship with a special woman. I started dating off and on, only to learn that dating is an expensive and frustrating process. People in L.A. come from many cultures and places. They bring with them ideals and

232

social differences that were minimally compatible with my own. I longed to find a partner who was compatible with my ideals and interests. Dating and trying to find the "right" woman was like looking for a needle in a hay stack. The dating process made me feel like I was wasting my time, money and energy. Many times I felt that I was better off alone.

One day I was reading an internet posted article about the dating process. The person who posted the article was Julie Ferman, an independent professional matchmaker and dating coach. I decided to check out Julie's website (www.julieferman.com) and see if her business model fit with my expectations. Julie owned a private database of single men and women. Her focus was finding the best possible introductions for each of her active search clients using her proprietary methodology, private database, and flexible stair-stepped fee structure. After meeting with Julie and talking about how she could help me find new love, I was convinced her business model was exactly what I needed. I signed up as a new personal matchmaking client and jumped into Julie's process. Not being in a hurry, I calculated it would take me two years or more to find the right person. I was looking for a one-on-one long-term relationship.

After eight months of dating through Julie's database I was ready to take three months off from the dating scene. Julie called and convinced me to read about her newest client before making a decision about taking time off. I became intrigued with Julie's newest client, and to my surprise, this new client turned out to be very interesting – I wanted to learn more about her. She lived in the local area, was a business technology professional and in search of a one-on-one long term relationship. Through Julie's matchmaking process we both agreed to meet at a local restaurant for a first date. The evening went quite well and we agreed to meet for a second date. The second date became a stepping stone to ongoing dates that led into an exclusive relationship. We felt that our exclusivity would give us an honest assessment of our relationship and help us determine if there were a future together.

One full year went by and we were still dating and becoming inseparable. The dating scene in L.A. had changed for me and was now exciting, joyous and filled with love. Together we enjoyed the many pleasures of what L.A. had to offer such as Hollywood entertainment, dining and non-stop outdoor activities. Another six months passed and our relationship had blossomed into inseparable love, mutual trust, faith and outstanding communication. We openly admitted our commitment to each other and decided some day we should seriously think about getting married. This was definitely another fork in the road for me. My risk management business, acting/modeling and personal life in L.A. was in full bloom. It felt like the sky was the limit and the future was what we would make of it.

Thoughts for You

Throughout my years as a professional actor and model, I learned that actors needed business smarts plus the ability to perform to be successful. As an independent actor living in L.A. and learning the entertainment industry on a day by day basis, business acumen was a must. If an actor was fortunate to have a close friend or family member in the business, he or she could be a gold mine of information to help maneuver the Hollywood trenches. If the actor didn't know anyone in the business, it was important to be surrounded with trusting and supporting friends, and/or a loving and supportive personal relationship. It's even more important to have a supportive base of people to help the actor manage through the constant rejection. Being rejected more times than one can count is difficult for most people. I witnessed countless actors and models (male and female) become mentally scarred or jaded about the business. Internalizing and holding onto the mental scarring of constant rejection can have negative impacts on the attitude of a person.

When someone states that thick skin is required to make it in Hollywood, they are absolutely correct. The same goes for building a business. My thick skin was derived from life's lessons and my ability to be resilient through constant change. Putting yourself in the Hollywood scene on a full-time basis is like jumping into a large bowl of controlled chaos. You never know where you will be or what you will be doing from one day to the next. For me, when working in the midst of short-term chaos, I excelled. For others, they would crash and burn. Having a pre-planned strategy that included a career backup plan significantly helped me live through the uncertainty of the Hollywood spin cycle. I kept my focus on the future while tending to the day-to-day needs of paying the bills.

I believe that anyone who has the deep desire to make it in the entertainment industry should go for it one hundred ten percent. The entertainment industry is by far the most exhilarating, dynamic, and fun industry I have ever experienced. As with any powerful industry, it does have its pitfalls and shortcomings. The key is to have a long term

235

plan/vision while fully understanding and accepting that it could take five, ten, or fifteen years to be successful. Or, you may never achieve the success you originally dreamed. If you become wildly successful, major kudos to you! Everyone's success is measured and perceived differently. I believe I was successful. I didn't reach the apex of the A-list team, but I did earn my right to become a SAG/AFTRA professional actor and I booked myself a recurring role on a daytime soap opera. Through my risk management consulting business I earned enough money to pay my bills in an area identified as an excessively expensive place to live. I also found a new life-long love in my life.

There are a vast majority of entertainers who have paid their dues and worked their way up the Hollywood ladder. For those individuals who found success, most will tell you there were no short-cuts. The same is true in starting and growing your own business. Keeping your integrity, making yourself accountable, repeatedly getting back up after you have fallen (resilience), respecting the work and putting trust into the process are enablers to success. These slaughterhouse rules can help you be successful in your life, whether you choose the entertainment industry or another desired path.

*****

"Dream big and dare to fail." Norman Vaughan

Chapter 16 – For the Future

The Winds of Texas

My girlfriend was born and raised in L.A. However, her family was originally from Texas where she had family and friend roots. As a Southern California native she also had family, friend, and business relationships throughout the Southern California region. When we met she was returning from a one year sabbatical between jobs and had begun networking with her professional contacts. She successfully landed a management consulting position with a company whose corporate office was located in L.A.

During the month of October, 2009 I asked her to marry me (she said yes). Our original plan was to marry between April and July, 2010. However, both of our daughters had other plans: they were pregnant and their due dates fell within the same time frame as our desired wedding date. To work with everyone's calendar's, we ended up targeting a wedding date for mid-December, 2009. My fiancé was traveling quite a bit for business which made our situation a bit nerve-racking. With just two months to plan and prepare the rush was on to get married. We had a fun time planning the wedding and getting our family members excited about our upcoming date. Mid-December came upon us very quickly and as planned, we held a small family-only garden wedding at my fiancés home. Upon return from our honeymoon I moved out of my home and into my wife's home. From that point forward my property became a one hundred percent rental property, and as newlyweds, we focused on our joint life together and future goals.

The company my wife consulted for had privately stated they were planning to move their corporate office from L.A. to Irving, Texas (a suburb area between Dallas and Fort Worth in northern Texas). The corporate move would not be completed for one full year. Inside this transition period, my wife started traveling to/from Dallas and L.A. to help ensure their IT department was well prepared for the big transition. Throughout 2010 and 2011 my wife was spending every work week in Irving and the weekends in L.A. Then in March of 2012 my stepdaughter and her family moved from Tennessee into a new home in the Dallas, Texas area. All of a sudden, there was talk inside the family about everything Texas had to offer. My wife and I began discussing a possible dual property selloff and move from L.A. to the Dallas area. It seemed like the eastward blowing winds were pushing us toward the state of Texas. Of course, this would be another impactful transition in my life.

The recession between 2008 and 2012 had taken its toll on my risk management consulting and advisory business. The recession wiped out my entire client base. I did manage, however, to pick up two new small projects along the west coast. These two new clients paid the bills but nothing more. My acting career was somewhat flat and I began to seriously think about my long term plan towards financial freedom.

The State of Texas showed greater job prospects in the risk management industry plus we had family living in the Dallas area. With a possible Texas move I had to accept the fact that my acting career would suffer. Texas is a right to work state which means fewer union vs. non-union jobs. My wife and I had many discussions about the minimal

238

acting possibilities in Texas. With her full love and support we agreed that our best action plan was to look east and start planning for a major life change. Again, a fork in the road presented itself. It was time to pick up the fork, put it in my pocket and move forward with the winds of Texas at my back.

The Big Sell Off and Move

Together we embraced a new and exciting plan. My wife was going to sell her property, I would sell my property and we would move into a newly purchased home in the Dallas/Ft. Worth area. Sounds easy enough – doesn't it? The entire process was a ton of work and it took the better part of two years to complete.

First, we had to prepare my wife's property for sale. This meant finding a realtor, getting advice for pre-sale and then prepping the property for the market. My wife had been living in her home for twenty eight years so there was plenty of work to do prior to the big sale. I spent four months prepping the house and its surrounding property. We obtained the green light from our realtor to put the property up for sale. Our plan was to live in my house while we sold my wife's house. During this prep period of my wife's property, I gave my tenants a three month notice to vacate my property. The move back to my property required renting a storage facility and turning my garage into a temporary storage facility too. With the much appreciated help of friends and family, we successfully moved the majority of my wife's furniture and other personal possessions into a storage facility and my garage – whew!

I began taking trips to Dallas where my wife and I looked at homes with a Dallas realtor, who showed us many wonderful properties in targeted surrounding communities. Our goal was to leverage the sale of my wife's property to help purchase a home somewhere close to her family. After months of searching and traveling back and forth, we couldn't find just the right property that provided the privacy and location we desired. Our plan changed from purchasing an existing home to finding a lot and building our own place. We realized that building a home together would make it "our" nest, no more his house/her house. We found a residential acreage that fit our desires, location, and budget. We wrote a check and temporarily secured the land for our purchase. Back in L.A. the housing industry had turned the corner and was now a seller's market.

During the recession mortgage interest rates were very low and hovering around four percent. All of a sudden renters with two incomes could afford to purchase a home in the expensive L.A. market. With a large enough down payment, their monthly mortgage payment could equal what they paid for in rent. Our realtor predicted a competitive sale of my wife's property. Their assessment was correct and we had multiple offers. My wife's property sold within thirty days. This allowed us to put earnest money down to begin building our new home. We hired a local Texas professional home builder and began designing a home together that we could call our own.

The sale of my wife's property was complete and the process of designing and building our new home had begun. It was time to start prepping my property for sale. For five years I had put some serious sweat equity into the house, garage, lot and swimming pool area. The real estate market was heavily primed for the seller and my property was the next bulls-eye for sale. Our realtor predicted a fast and competitive sale – it was. At the same time, the building of our new home in Texas was on schedule with a targeted move-in date of May, 2013. The trick was selling and then moving out of my house at about the same time our new home in Texas was ready to be inhabited. I began the process of prepping my property for sale while attempting to time the sale and move to match the build schedule of our new home. The timing worked out perfectly. Within the first two weeks of living in our new home in North Texas, my property in L.A. was sold at above the asking price and we put the proceeds into the new home.

Getting Re-established

Moving to the Dallas/Ft. Worth area was exciting and filled with promise. It did, however, come with one underestimated major drawback. I didn't know a single person in the metropolitan area. In fact, I didn't know anybody "professionally" in the State of Texas! This meant starting all over building my professional and personal network. Starting from scratch takes a considerable amount of time and energy. It took about two months to get situated into our new home. The garage was filled with boxes and the property needed constant attending and management. When I had free time, I was searching for networking clubs and professional organizations that supported my career aspirations. I quickly learned about the good hearted people of Texas. People in the North Texas area went out of their way to help me connect with other professional colleagues. I was referred to organizations that required a personal referral to join. The warm generosity of the Texas people was a welcoming and wonderful experience.

Within the time period of moving to Texas the two contracts I had with my consulting company had reached their final conclusions. The time had come to "fire myself" and move toward a new future in the risk management industry. During the first week of May, 2013 with a heavy heart I legally dissolved the company. My new goal was to find full time or contract to hire employment in the business risk management industry. In the third quarter of 2013 there were plenty of non-managerial opportunities. However, as an ex-business owner and Chief Executive Officer (CEO) I was looking for a leadership position. I designed a new business card, re-worked my resume, and began the process of marketing and selling myself into the north Texas market. It took me about ten months to land my first full time position as a cybersecurity leader with a global corporation. The existing team of people were previously mismanaged, had little direction with mostly negative responses towards management. It was the type of challenge I was looking for as their new corporate leader. In five months I successfully gained their trust and started ten new security projects that were aligned with business objectives. These successes were accomplished by implementing the slaughterhouse rules of accountability, integrity, resilience, respect, and trust.

I spent one year at my new corporate position only to learn the company was being purchased by a much larger global corporation. Apparently, the "big gorilla" wanted to expand their market share while joining the ranks of companies offering cloud services to business customers. The corporate decision makers were located on the east coast. This business model did not fit well with the company leadership team located in the Dallas/Ft. Worth area. The entire local management team was asked to leave the company and given reduction in force financial packages. Once again I found myself in the ranks of the unemployed but in an industry that had more job openings than security professionals to fill them. It was time to re-evaluate my career position and move forward with new opportunities.

The Security Industry Gets Hot

With a new life in North Texas, my focus was building on my current cybersecurity and risk management knowledge, expertise, and education. I had eleven years of experience in the risk management business, two certifications (Certified Chief Information Security Officer – CCISO and Certified Information Systems Security Professional – CISSP) under my belt, two college degrees (Bachelor of Science Electronics Engineering Technology – BSEET and Masters of Technology Management – MoTM), and strong knowledge of the risk management industry as a whole.

For eleven years I had witnessed the increase in bad actors (hackers/criminals) stealing intellectual property and proprietary data (electronic information) from well-known businesses throughout the world. The internet that I had helped build was being used against us at an alarming rate. The dot.com bubble burst in 2000 and the Great Recession which hit in the wake of the sub-prime mortgage crisis of

2007/2008, was so financially impacting that companies initiated massive layoffs and cut spending to survive. Unfortunately the spending cuts included zero to minimal investment in risk management services and cybersecurity solutions. This created fertile ground for the criminals to steal data at will. Public and private companies were racing to purchase the next best tool or application that promised to keep criminals out of their networks. On average the criminals were stealing data for eight months before technical staff inside companies realized they were getting ripped off. To keep up with demand venture capitalists and private equity investors were investing tens of billions of dollars into the cybersecurity startup industry. The security industry became the hottest world-wide job market. It was a whole new world in risk management with plenty of opportunity to excel in my risk management career.

The security industry was growing without bounds and quickly facing growing pains. In just a few years a major shortage of skilled internet technologists, programmers and information security people had developed. If felt like there were five jobs for every security professional. In the United States alone, there were an estimated two hundred twenty five thousand unfilled security positions. Worldwide the estimate was approximately two million. New start-up security businesses were being developed every hour of every day. Investment money was flowing rapidly into the security sector, and enterprises of every size were buying security technology faster than availability from manufacturers. This newly formed industry felt very much like the internet boom of the nineties. The questions in my mind were, how long will it last and when will the security bubble burst?

Empirical Data and the Art of Knowing

From 1990 through the year 2001 I had experienced a very similar rise in a technology enabled industry (the buildout of the internet). During the internet boom there were more jobs than qualified people to fill them. The boom created a plethora of new technology vendors vying for customers. From that experience, I learned to think more critically about the many technologies being sold to businesses. When I was a systems engineer, I believed that without our support for implementing technology, businesses would fail. I was headstrong into technology and believed technology was the panacea to everything that ailed businesses. When I became a business owner, I quickly realized that successful businesses operate within a triangle. The triangle is people, process and technology. I learned that technology is an enabler to doing business but is not the end all problem solution for businesses. During the internet boom, I witnessed many technology enabled projects fail to achieve their calculated Return on Investment (ROI).

The cybersecurity industry is no different. This new industry is built on the knowledge of people, effective business processes, and enabling technology. People are the most expensive asset inside businesses, and they are the most valuable asset too. Just like the internet boom, without a knowledgeable and well-educated workforce, security technology would become a financial ball and chain around the neck of senior management. Every day I would read about another company

245

getting its network breached by a new strain of malicious software (malware). Thinking back when I was working as a network systems engineer or architect, I don't ever remember talking with my colleagues about securing the communication systems being deployed to buildout the Internet. The Internet I remember building did not openly support or integrate detailed and functional security controls. There were, however, firewall appliances being deployed. The initial intent of the corporate firewall was to disallow fellow employees searching the Internet for pornographic material. We didn't talk about securing the plethora of business applications being implemented worldwide. This meant that millions of software based applications had been developed and implemented with very little information security in mind. The software was filled with a seemingly endless supply of weak security controls or none at all. The hackers were having a field day by breaching companies all across the globe.

Another primary security threat to businesses and their adjoining services was the insider threat. The recession cost millions of people their jobs. This created enhanced employee dissent, disappointment, and dismay throughout corporate America. Employees, from executives to system administrators, were being targeted by criminals to steal and sell company secrets. These trusted employees had direct access to company intellectual property. This new digital information could easily find its way onto laptops, thumb drives or smart phones. Via the deep dark web this digital information could be sold to eagerly awaiting criminal sources. Never before in the history of human information management had so much intellectual property been stolen and re-purposed for ill intent. Clearly, the security industry was well behind the demand of the black market. Inclusive of security practitioners lagging behind criminal activity, businesses of all types and sizes were slow to invest in high-tech security solutions. It would take many years for the security industry's technology-based solutions to manifest themselves as viable business investments. In fact, this business problem still persists today.

In a very strange way, the internet work I performed in the nineties has given my security career a whole new beginning. It feels like I was an integral part of creating problems (the Internet with minimal security), then developing the security solutions to fix the problems I created. All the while I was earning a living on both sides of the fence. I am fortunate to live in a metropolitan area that is bringing in new business and supporting established businesses that built the local economy. The security industry is red hot in North Texas with plenty of opportunity. However, with opportunity comes career risk. During the Internet buildout frenzy I would accept the next job that offered a greater salary with a higher position. From those earlier experiences, I learned that when it came to my career path, sometimes short-term financial gain would manifest itself into long-term career pain. This time I decided to take my time by assessing and re-evaluating my entire career position. It was time for a one-year sabbatical and the development of a revised action plan.

I promised myself and my family that my new long-term career action plan would focus on achieving a leadership position in the security industry. My new action plan consisted of identifying where, when and how I wanted my working career to be in one, three, five years

247

and beyond. I decided it was time to put myself back into the contracting market and become an integral part of the "gig economy." From previous experience I learned that contracting created a flexible work schedule which I truly enjoyed. Besides, I had the opportunity to provide outstanding information security leadership value to new client prospects across multiple industries.

As an information systems security professional, I have had the opportunity to work in different environments and companies. This type of work is very exciting, challenging, and comes with constant learning curves. From college, I remember that the more I learned, the more I realized how much more there was to learn. The same is true when contracting in the security industry. It has become a very fast moving industry with plenty of problems to solve. With the support of my family and having a career action plan targeted for the cybersecurity industry, I have greater opportunity for success with achieving my short and long term career goals and objectives. Ultimately, I believe these goals and objectives will allow me to live a well-rounded life that supports my family and successfully achieve financial freedom.

Thoughts for You

When I moved to L.A. to pursue an acting career and build on my risk management business, I never thought I would end up finding new love, moving to Texas and becoming a successful information security leader. On a personal level I knew at some future time I would search for new love. However, I did not know if I would ever find a new life partner and accepted the fact that I would be single for many, many years. I had absolutely no idea that a far reaching global recession would positively impact my future financial position. It never occurred to me that I would be making another big move and change in my life.

Moving to Texas and leaving behind an industry of possibilities was challenging yet filled with new unknown opportunities. Fortunately, I had help from loving family and friends. Without their love and support my transition to a new life in Texas would never have gone so well. This life experience is a true testament that it takes a village to be successful with life's endeavors.

Looking back at my life in L.A. there were many challenges and constant change. The entertainment industry required flexibility, team spirit, independence, specificity, yet openness to meet the needs of working as an actor. The risk management industry requires much of the same. Can you find similar parallels across your personal or work life? Can you identify specific areas in your life today that challenge you as an individual or team player? Will the winds of change move you toward a new or changing life fulfilling purpose or leave you empty without direction or hope? Sometimes all that is required is the willingness to allow change and opportunity to happen with you, not against you.

*****

"You are the CEO of your life." James M. Myers

Epilogue

Since my early days, as the youngest starting pitcher on a baseball team, I saw myself as a leader of some kind. That internal view of my passion and talent became stronger as I later directed laborers on a construction site, picked up a clipboard in my Navy days, and ultimately became a CEO of my own company. Throughout the course of my life, I have found myself most satisfied in leadership positions. Was I in search of these positions or did others see something unbeknownst to myself? I believe everyone has some type of positive strength qualities within them and for some, it requires being placed in a position to show inner passion, learning potential, or simply the desire to move forward. For others, such as myself, it was the support of a mentor in the workplace. This is all part of the never ending life cycle of change and opportunity.

For the many life impacting forks in the road I have come across in my life, none of the life impacting decisions was easy. An important aspect of making work or personal life decisions is positioning yourself so that a decision can or must be made. If you are thinking about making a change in your life, put together a plan. Then frame the alternatives and move toward making the decision, armed with the pros and cons, as well as an understanding of its context in your plan. For every single fork in the road, there were multiple paths leading to it. Ask yourself how you arrived where you are today? Why are you in this situation? Am I committed to following through with a difficult decision? When I make this decision, where do I see myself in one, three, or five years and beyond? With an action plan in hand, answers to these types of questions can be answered.

I have found that having a plan helped me maneuver life's events and unexpected changes. Don't be afraid to reflect on your goals and new opportunities or setbacks while working your plan and growing toward your potential. You can always change or update the plan as necessary, because, your life has not been carved in stone. As a human being, you are capable of making wonderful changes and improvements in your life. You have the ability to pick up a fork in the road, put it in your pocket, and move toward a better life for yourself, your family, and friends. It may not be easy, and there will be challenges. There may be the lowest of lows and the highest of highs. You can develop your own set of "rules" or you can engage with the slaughterhouse rules. Whichever rules you live by, they can become your baseline towards building a life greater than you ever dreamed.

Writing this book has re-enforced my faith in God and country, and my appreciation for the love and support of my family. Coupled with living by the slaughterhouse rules, my life is fulfilling far and above what I thought possible. If I can do it, then yes, I believe you can do it too.

About the Author

James Myers is an independent author, business entrepreneur, cybersecurity professional, actor, veteran, and most importantly, the grandfather to six beautiful grandchildren. James currently lives in the North Texas region of the United States with his beloved wife. He's an avid golfer, enjoys weight training, reading, and traveling.

Connect with the author at http://www.slaughterhouserules.com

Made in the USA
Columbia, SC
06 March 2020